Imagine

CW00420725

Imagine a guidebook to Leeds in the year 2100. I have no doubt that close to the top of the section on unmissable attractions will be the Leeds Tapestry. Even today the Leeds Tapestry is clearly an extraordinary work of art but as each year goes by its importance and stature will be increasingly acclaimed.

It succeeds splendidly in being a visual record of the history and evolution of a great city and, at the same time, being a contemporary record of the vitality of Leeds at the start of the twenty first century. A picture tells a thousand stories, they say, and in the panels of the tapestry we can all recognise many familiar aspects of life in Leeds today. For most of us too the images stimulate special resonances associated with our lives and those of friends and colleagues.

Kate Russell's vision in embarking on the tapestry was audacious, and it has taken a small army of volunteers and sheer dogged determination to see it through. As a project almost entirely the result of volunteer labour and private and personal sponsorship, the Tapestry is an outstanding example of civic pride. We all have good reason to congratulate Kate and the hundreds of volunteers on their great skill and commitment. We must also warmly thank all the Tapestry's sponsors for having the confidence and foresight to support this important venture.

This book is a celebration of the Leeds Tapestry; of this great shared enterprise. Future generations of Leeds citizens and visitors to the city will marvel at the

Dr. Kevin Grady, Director of Leeds Civic Trust, presents Kate Russell with her Spirit of Leeds Award 2000 finalists trophy for her sterling work on the Leeds Tapestry.
Photo: Martin Banks

intricacy of the panels and the stories that they tell. Happily for them, and indeed for us, they will be able to consult this extremely attractive book telling them how the tapestry was made. Many will have the great pleasure of being able to say with immense pride that a relative of theirs helped create it.

Kevin Grady

KEVIN GRADY

Director
Leeds Civic Trust

Although, throughout my childhood and adolescence, my Grandmother made me beautifully smocked dresses and exquisite tatted lace collars, needlework first entered my life only in 1964 when I was expecting my son, Mark. Things went badly wrong so that I had to spend the last three months of my pregnancy in bed in order to prevent a premature birth. I was not at all ill so that passing the time became more and more difficult; one cannot read all the time after all.

One day a friend arrived bearing wool, canvas and needles. "This will keep you sane!" she said, and she was right.

The therapy provided by needlework is, to me, more valuable than any other: no drugs, no expense (apart from the materials), the benefit from keeping one's hands occupied while one's mind is free, plus the fact that, with any luck and a bit of skill, the end product will be something of beauty which will last for many hundreds of years. Needlework has seen me through all kinds of crises from delayed flights (your paperback will run out but not your needlework!), union disputes when my husband was running English National Opera, family divorces and baby dramas to breast cancer, and is a wonderful thing to do while listening to music on gramophone records or the radio.

Therapy apart, the sheer discipline necessitated by needlework extends to the mind as well as to the fingers. To hurry inevitably means bad work, unpicking and repetition so that very soon one learns to take the work at its own pace. Once this lesson has been learnt it becomes part of one's mental process as well as a physical one and goes hand in hand with reflection, contemplation and even praying. The free mind is not necessarily a vacant one!

This House is full of needlework, not of course on the scale of Hardwick Hall in Derbyshire with its extraordinary collection of antique embroideries, but significant just the same as a piece of social history. There are Chippendale chairs still with their original needlework covers. Many other chairs can be found throughout the House, both in the rooms open to the public and our private apartments. Alas seldom signed or dated, which is a pity as it would be nice to be able to place the embroiderer responsible, and, for instance, to know which Lady Harewood it was who thought no one would ever see the back of her work and who, when wanting to work in a different area, simply brought her needle up wherever she chose, regardless of the untidy cats cradle of unsecured threads this produced on the back of the canvas.

Almost every country has produced highly individual and characteristic needlework for many centuries. One of the most fascinating to me is India which continues to be an unrivalled source of delight and inspiration in this regard. India is short neither of willing

H.M. The Queen visiting Harewood House on the occasion of the Golden Jubilee. H.M. The Queen and Lady Harewood are both looking at the Leeds in Bloom panel with Kate Russell.
Photo: Hicks Photography

hands nor time so the stream of beautiful and intricate embroidery is never-ending. My husband and I sit each evening facing a magnificent though faded Indian bed cover which we have as a wall-hanging, with elephants and peacocks, worked in gold laid work and silk on a navy blue wool cloth, processing around the sides through a riot of flowers and birds. Over many years I have also collected beautifully embroidered caftans and table mats with work fine enough to send one blind. I have an enormous thinly woven woollen shawl almost too large to wear, which is intricately embroidered all over with leaves and tendrils which look the same on both sides. It must have taken an army of workers of the highest quality to do it!

In the bigger picture tapestry has always had a vital role in history. The Bayeux Tapestry and the stunningly beautiful Apocalypse Tapestries in the Chateau at Angers in the Loire (the earliest extant tapestry, finished in 1383, it is over 100 yards long and 20 feet high) remain perhaps the most spectacular examples of narrative illustrated by embroidery in the world. Happily, the tradition continues, not least in the country of my birth, Australia, where, in Melbourne there is a famous Tapestry Workshop which I love to visit on my trips home. I remember on one occasion seeing them copy a painting by the great Australian artist Arthur Boyd and being amazed at the effect the new medium had upon the work, the same of course, but very different with a heightened intensity of colour brought about by the wool.

Some years ago a group in Glasgow produced a wonderfully vivid work with whole-hearted and enlightened support, both financial and psychological, from the local council.

There is a most interesting book on the subject entitled Glasgow in Stitches telling the whole story of the huge amount of imagination, resourcefulness and skill.

Our own Leeds Millennium Tapestry has now been completed after years of hard work by many hundreds of volunteers under the inspirational leadership of the brilliant and redoubtable Kate Russell who has been responsible for the idea, its design and its execution. However, to me, the word completed is not correct. Why should this wonderful work ever be complete? As Leeds moves on, why should we not make more panels as a continuing record of our city and its people?

We have exhibited the Tapestry here at Harewood all this Summer and, even though we expected that it would engender keen interest, have been amazed by the enthusiasm from the large numbers who have visited it. In fact, so great has this been that we have had to extend the exhibition until mid-September.

After this it goes to the Armouries in Leeds. Then, who knows? The Tapestry needs a permanent and secure home where not only will it be properly cared for but also where the people of Leeds can easily see it. No solution has yet been found to this problem. Ideas for its solution would be gratefully received!

In the mean time let us all simply enjoy the fruits of the labour of the many hundreds from all races and walks of life who united in celebrating the city in which we all take pride, Leeds.

THE COUNTESS OF HAREWOOD
Volunteer & Patron of the Leeds Tapestry

How We Made It

KATE RUSSELL INTERVIEWED BY HEATHER DIXON

INSPIRATION AND VISION

"Art that matters to people delights the senses, moves the heart, revives the soul and offers courage for living."

Such simple words, yet so inspirational. For it was this extract from anthropologist Lewis Hyde's celebrated book *The Gift: Imagination and the Erotic Life of Property* which became one of the catalysts of the Leeds Tapestry and the essence of a project which was to become much more than an extraordinary work of art. It would become a major conversation piece - not just among those who came to see it, but for those who were to follow Kate Russell's innovative way of working - a way of working which was based primarily on conversations.

As a self-employed artist Kate had been working for some years with individuals, groups and companies to co-create 'Conversation Pieces'. She held a very successful exhibition in 1986 at the Manor House Gallery, Ilkley showing a selection of commissioned works produced in this way.

Through talking to people at length, she embarked on a fascinating voyage of discovery. As conversations developed and deepened, they produced a rich seam of ideas which not only challenged her own perceptions but also resulted in an art work that had meaning for both parties...each had a sense of 'ownership' of the end result.

"In this way, appreciation and greater awareness for both the object and the creative process is developed which can provide openings for new and richer ways of perceiving the world," said Kate.

Conversation wasn't the only source of inspiration for the Tapestry. Visual impact generated by the twelve vivid banners created with the community by Claire Higney of Needleworks – *Keeping Glasgow in Stitches (1990)*, also came into the mix. So did Kate's participation in the Leeds Common Purpose Programme, which encourages people to develop ideas within the community and across all sectors, regenerating the idea of citizenship.

Taking all these influences on board, Kate - the Tapestry's creator and director - visualised a major work which would draw together people from all walks of life who could contribute to something which would be displayed to visitors from all over the world.

The result of that dream is extraordinary.

"One of the aims of the Tapestry was to raise the profile of textile art, which is greatly underestimated in our culture", said Kate. "Textile art which is appreciated in other cultures is undervalued in ours and Leeds has no great civic tapestry even though much of the city's wealth and culture

The Team stitching down sections on *Community Spirit.*

How We Made It

KATE RUSSELL INTERVIEWED BY HEATHER DIXON

was built on a combination of textiles and engineering. Most people glaze over when you mention embroidery, but when they see something like this they can immediately relate to it. It's a cross between a flat image and a sculpture. There is a richness to it, a tactile sensuality. It has integrity. It activates the mind, the heart and the soul. I am reminded of the Indian myth in which the threads of the tapestry are like structures of the universe and the stitches going in and out represent the journey of people's lives."

How fitting, then, that one volunteer returned home to India to share Kate's vision with her local community.

"I visited families of craftsmen in Mumbai and showed them postcards of the Tapestry. There were about seven young boys, aged 10 to 15, sitting around a frame doing embroidery on the same piece. They became interested in our project and explained that in families of artisans, master craftsmen teach the boys embroidery at a very young age.
There is still a considerable demand for this work so traditional embroidery is very much alive all over India."
Ayesha Dost, Volunteer.

The Leeds Tapestry is now a remarkable example of what can be achieved through the combined powers of highly motivated individuals, extraordinary team-work and one woman's dream. This montage of millions of stitches, depicting the past, present and future of a community which goes from strength to strength, has been hailed as one of the finest examples of collaborative embroidery in the world and an extraordinary slice of modern history.

IN THE BEGINNING

Kate's origins contributed to her deep interest in the arts. "Textiles and making something out of nothing was a part of my childhood," she said. "Both my parents worked in the Yorkshire woollen mills and then it was something I wanted to get away from. When I went to art college I thought I had escaped from everything associated with poverty and the limitations of my past, but eventually my hands and eyes drew me back to textiles, now perceived from a different point of view. Art opened my eyes and mind to infinite possibilities and I love to share that 'wonder' with others.

"My mother was a great knitter. During the war when it was difficult to get materials she would unravel part-worn jumpers and pull old clothes apart and make new ones, so it was rather ironic when I finally came full circle and found a fascination for yarns and materials and fabrics. Now I really appreciate the time she spent with me teaching me to knit and to make clothes for my dolls. Making things and the whole creative process has helped me through bleak times, put things in perspective and given me something to work for. Now I'm seeing it do the same sort of thing for others, and it's a wonderful feeling."

CREATIVE PROCESSES

"One of the obvious ways to show the delights of textile art to people was to use as many different techniques as possible in constructing the Tapestry," said Kate. "Unlike many civic tapestry projects, which

employed experienced needleworkers, I hoped that people of all skill levels from beginners to professionals would participate and learn from each other."

"We have used so many techniques in the making of the Tapestry, yet a lot of these could be lost in our country if we are not careful. It's important that we pass on our skills as much as we possibly can".

Gill Cook, Volunteer.

"In *The Gift* Lewis Hyde talks about the 'group mind', the synergy of working creatively with other people. It is difficult to describe the many creative threads that linked all the volunteer embroiderers with the central design process and with each other. This was the heart of the project – the myriad practical and intuitive ways in which working with others towards a shared goal extends everyone's creativity."

"Kate makes volunteers feel they are the only ones who can do a particular piece. It's encouraging and gives people a new perspective of their own abilities – the confidence that they can do whatever they want to do".

Barbara Walker, a Trustee of the charity and computer archivist.

"You see the flaws in your work which other people don't see, so you need someone to reassure you sometimes and say, 'It's fine'."

Renee Silverman, Volunteer and Tapestry Minute Secretary.

"When I lost my husband after a long illness, the Tapestry became a great healer for me. I needed incentive to

keep going. I not only got that, but I also gained a whole new circle of friends. When my husband died I was left in an abyss. The Tapestry filled it again."

The late Audrey Pidgeon, Volunteer.

"I worked on the Queen's Hotel which I remember being opened when I was a very small girl. I was very much in awe of this enormous white building. I never did manage to count how many windows I embroidered."

Audrey Gabbitas, Volunteer.

"I saw the Leeds Tapestry 2000 project as a way of keeping textile skills alive - including mine. I believe when you retire it's important to use your brain. They say, 'If you don't use it, you'll lose it'."

Betty Bertrand, Volunteer and Trustee.

"I started my own business and found that you didn't actually have conversations with clients – you just dealt with the matter in hand, so it was very lonely. Coming to the group meant I could laugh and talk informally again. It was a great way to unwind and to feel part of a team again."

Freda Copley, Volunteer.

"Thanks to the Tapestry I feel more settled, more confident - the 'real me' - after several traumas. Now I've been asked to design a tapestry for Horbury, where I live."

Janet Taylor, Volunteer.

MAKING IT HAPPEN

The first volunteers identified themselves in February 1993 at a meeting of the Embroiderers' Guild. Sue Hodgson was the first to begin embroidery and she and

Audrey Gabbitas, Chair of the Yorkshire Branch of the Guild, attended the first meeting of potential sponsors at the office of Booth & Co Solicitors (later Addleshaw Booth). The idea was to show the assembled legal sector professionals how the proposed Tapestry could look and the diversity of textile techniques. The intention was to find out a) if firms would be interested in sponsoring a section representing their business and b) if any individuals would be interested in learning or developing their needlework skills.

"Textile art is a difficult medium to talk about," Kate said. "If you cannot experience the tangible sensual, tactile elements of saturated colour with an added dimension, it is almost impossible to comprehend. Until we had finished examples of embroidery, we had to rely on slides, enthusiasm and the wonderful raw materials of our trade."

Her enthusiasm rubbed off and she soon found herself with a small army of volunteers who were invited to meetings, fund raising lunches and events to help to raise interest not only in the Tapestry project itself, but the textile arts generally.

She also managed to set the sponsorship ball rolling with gusto.

As with the volunteers, Kate's intention was that all the sponsors would get some value out of participation with the Tapestry project. Not only would the process be interesting and interactive for both Directors and employees, but it would also produce a unique image for use in publicity and TV and other media coverage.

Sponsor participation was essential. In fact the majority of ideas in the panels were provided in conversation or correspondence with the individuals and organisations represented. Many photographs, original and valuable documents, paintings and drawings were provided by the sponsoring companies. They also made very welcome recommendations to other colleagues and invitations for Tapestry staff and volunteers to events where we could meet potential sponsors.

For the first few years Kate did all the fund-raising with her husband Brian's help. Barbara Cresswell, who had worked at Wheatfields Hospice raising funds for many years, lent Kate her expertise for two days a week for nearly two years, until she finally retired in December 1996. Nicki Martineau stepped in for six months and then, in mid-1997, Sylvia Crowther, the project's only employee, took the reins, finding contacts, arranging meetings and following up promises. Sometimes there would be an awfully long gap between a promise and the cheque – long enough for the company to change hands so that the whole process had to begin again.

In 1996 a committee of enthusiasts of the

106.
Mr G O'Donnell
Jackie Ford

Charting and stitching needlepoint at Armley Mills Museum.

Tapestry was founded which achieved charitable status for the project in 1997 when the committee became a Board of Trustees. This helped a great deal when applying for funding from other charitable bodies.

As the project grew so did the management costs and towards the end the annual sum needed to keep it afloat was around £60,000 which went towards office overheads, consultants' fees, materials, framing, photography, exhibitions costs, printing and insurance.

By the end of 1999 the project was in deeper financial difficulties than ever before and Kate and Sylvia turned to their many sponsors, friends and patrons for help and advice.

"The Countess of Harewood gave us a substantial donation and also steered us successfully through the process of applying for an award from the Peter Moores Foundation. This major award was sufficient, together with some of the other generous donations (listed on page 142) to give the project another year of life in which to complete the work." The 600 sponsors of panel sections contributed the majority of the £500,000 raised over ten years. Most of the headaches were around revenue funding and when sponsors made donations for the whole project or there was a successful application for funds from Trusts and Foundations, it gave a real boost to everyone.

Imagine, then, everyone's complete amazement when an anonymous donation of £20,000 arrived in 1997. This came at a time when the project was expanding beyond its means and provided resources to enable us to be more creative then just making ends meet. Moreover the benefits extended wider than the financial, giving us the moral support and assurance that we must be doing something worthwhile to counter the many criticisms we received.

LOGISTICS

In the beginning, when the volunteers numbered under a hundred, keeping in touch was relatively easy. As the project expanded and there were 300 or so on the mailing list, it was more difficult to keep the 'team' together (even if only half were 'active' at any one time.) Regular newsletters were one way of staying in touch but mostly Kate spent her evenings and weekends on the telephone, receiving and giving support, advice and encouragement or desperately seeking someone to embroider the gasworks!

There were hundreds of volunteers in non-embroidering capacities too. People who did hours of research, computer or hand charting, scanning images, proof-reading, sorting, tidying, cleaning, packing, transporting, stewarding at exhibitions and displays, giving slide talks, typing, filing photographs etc., not to mention the very important job of 'Tea Monitor' at all the workshops.

"I came on board in an advisory capacity because I have such a fascination for Leeds and its history. What I really enjoyed was meeting people I had known for years but never realised they were involved in a project like this. The difficulty is to know where to stop. There is always so much more you could do".

Robin Dove, Local Historian.

Many volunteers didn't know where to stop and found their lives taken over. Barbara Walker, for example, gave thousands of hours of time over a period of six years, mostly at the computer. Betty Bertrand's many skills led her to diversify from embroidery to Chairmanship, organising stewards, stock control and managing the finances. Ruth Fowler gave slide talks about the Tapestry for over six years, not only recruiting volunteers and sponsors but also raising funding. Glynis Evans, Janet Taylor, Beverley and Renee Silverman also gave talks to spread the word about the project.

Kate aimed not only to bring excellence and diversity to the techniques used in the Tapestry but also to create a valuable and creative educational experience for the volunteers. To this end she organised high quality, art college level tuition with artists of national and international renown.

"Kate invited well-established artists to run master classes and workshops – not only were these tutors inspiring, but the work on the Tapestry that they

stimulated – embracing every kind of fibre art, gave me complete freedom to work in my own way. The two people who inspired me most were Claire Bryan and Paddy Killer. Their influence on my work was unmatched."
Anne Cove, Volunteer.

"I have always believed that people can do anything given the right circumstances and encouragement and the confidence to try things for themselves. I saw myself as a facilitator rather than a teacher."
**Sarah Hodgson,
Volunteer and Workshop Leader.**

Kate also found the workshops inspiring. "Seeing another artist's work and discovering not only how it was produced but what led to that particular interpretation is a great way to learn. To be with others making these discoveries, sharing the delight in mutual accomplishment, opens doors to more adventurous and innovative ways of working."

"There was a real feel of trail blazing, because everyone was always looking one step ahead and wanting to try something they had never done before. I did the judges and I managed to get hold of some horse-hair for the wigs, but the cat got hold of it and I found it spread all the way round the house. I had to go round after it picking up every piece of horse hair individually."
**Gillian Kempner,
Volunteer and Trustee.**

"The Tapestry gave us a whole new

Workshop at Armley Mills Museum.

Kate stitching sections of *Civic Pride*.

Betty Bertrand working on *Jack Higgins.*

insight into Leeds. Take the architecture, for instance. Usually you walk down the street and never bother to glance up at the buildings around you, but when you are working on a project like this it makes you take notice of the tiniest details and to really appreciate the city in which you live."

Freda Copley, Volunteer.

"Kate suggested different techniques and approaches but didn't force ideas on us – she more or less let us do what we wanted – I'm sure that is why we have such a vast and interesting selection of embroideries on the panels – using peoples' own ideas."

Eileen Wilson, Volunteer.

"There were dozens of workshops just to make the leaves. Some leaves were even done in Wales and posted to us". One day two women came to make tea for one of the workshops we were holding and they ended up embroidering leaves – no-one escaped!"

Shirley Gale, Volunteer.

Materials were of course provided, but many embroiderers supplied them from their own stocks or bought them as another form of donation. Equipment such as sewing machines, computers and magnifying lamps, were loaned to volunteers either short or long term and the project benefited enormously from exquisite needleworks, a fantastic image data base and skill-sharing days.

Kate also wanted to keep a record of every volunteer and every piece, so the work did not become anonymous as is so much historic embroidery. When Kate obtained

the first feasibility study funding from Leeds City Council and Yorkshire Arts in 1992/93, her first purchase was a huge ledger in which everyone involved could log what they had done. When this proved ineffective the group turned to project briefs and workshop registers and finally, after becoming computerised in 1998/99, every piece of embroidery was scanned and the details with it recorded.

From 1992 to 1995 the work space for both making the panels and for running workshops was in Kate Russell's home-based studio in Chapel Allerton. At the same time there was a display space and drop-in centre in the Victoria Quarter, where work was occasionally done to help involve the public in the process.

"The atmosphere in Kate's studio was incredible. It was really sunny and the frame took over the whole of the room. People were coming out of holes in the walls! The kettle was constantly on the boil and there were always vats of soup on the go to keep us going. I remember taking my baby daughter and thinking she would get trodden on if I put her on the floor, so I put her under the table in her car seat and she slept soundly through all the activity going on above her."

Gillian Kempner,
Volunteer and Trustee.

The offer of the Burling and Mending room in Armley Mills Museum was well timed, providing storage for the fast growing archive of design and research materials as well as housing the panels in progress and creating a space for technique workshops and meetings.

During the middle years of the project, fourteen panels were on the production line together, until it was decided to reduce the total number of panels to be produced to sixteen and amalgamate several themes into one, leaving us a mere twelve to complete.

The Burling and Mending room was used to produce the Tapestry panels for four years, though at times the project had to move its enormous collection of equipment and materials to other rooms in the museum, either because of essential repairs or the room was needed by another group.

"We were very happy working at Armley Mills – we even got used to the noise of the working looms – and so are delighted to show our appreciation in several sections of embroidery on the *Civic Pride, Pins and Needles, Community Spirit* and *Arts for All* panels," said Kate.

In 1999, with the help of Jane Hustwit, a then Trustee of the Tapestry, the Trustees were able to rent a larger room with additional storage space and security of tenure in the Holy Trinity Church on Boar Lane. This was a fantastic venue for people to 'drop in' whilst in town, but not so good for workshops as people could not drive up

to the door with heavy sewing machines or computers. Fortunately, the 'old faithful' volunteers kept up with the changes and a huge of amount of work was done here in the last few years. In all twelve panels were collated here, often with two frames on the working trestles at once.

IN THE DOLDRUMS

Between 1998 and 2000 the project moved location and offices four times, involved five new consultants and completely new computer technology, courtesy of the Arts Council Lottery. During this traumatic period, when production was at an all time low, the organisers managed to create several black holes into which valuable information disappeared, or was transmuted. There was a tide of complaints from volunteers that their newsletter had not arrived or we had the wrong name or address.

"In mid-1999, with only four panels completed, several of us were at our wits' end," said Kate. "I dreamt of emigrating and changing my name. It was painfully obvious that with only eighteen months to the end of the year 2000, the Tapestry would not be completed in time. Even with the reduced target of sixteen panels, it would take twenty-four years to complete the remaining twelve on past performance."

Alicia Foster and Pauline Idle selecting threads

The volunteers were becoming dispirited too. There was insufficient progress and too few embroidery projects as many of the panels were in stalemate awaiting sponsors. The initial target of twenty-four panels had gradually been reduced due to lack of financial support and themes were

Kate designing one of the panels.

amalgamated or abandoned altogether. This year was viewed by many as the lowest point of the project. It could only get better...and it did!

By late 1999 the volunteers using the equipment acquired through Arts Council Lottery funding were becoming much more familiar with the computers and sewing machines. There was an acceleration in the the training process and the level of production increased dramatically.

All the new consultants made great contributions (see p138) and Rosie Kearton, who joined in November 1999 as Project Co-ordinator, enabled Kate to get back to her main job of designing panels and sections and managing production of the Tapestry.

SUCCESS:

We made it! The last stitch in the fifteenth panel was put in at Holy Trinity Church on 19 April, 2002 and the entire project, office, workspace and store was moved back to the studio at 'The Elms'.

"In many ways the project has now come full circle and *Arts for All*, the remaining panel for us to complete, will be done by a reduced group of volunteers from my studio," said Kate. "We can now recapture the pioneering creative spirit with which we began and without the need to spend most of our time looking for funds. It is wonderful to have the thoughts and good wishes of the many thousands of people who have seen the fifteen panels displayed at Harewood House this summer."

"A vibrant commentary on a wonderful vibrant city."
Jean Jenkins, Collingham.

Margaret Chambers stitching *Education*.

The West Riding Ruggers.

"What can I say! No words could describe my amazement! Brilliant!!"
J Johnson, York.
"Wow! What amazing art. Such a high level of collaboration."
Kate Newton.

"It is lovely to see your own little piece of work made into something so good."
Karen Pattison, Volunteer.

"Very moving. The love and effort really shows."
Pauline Dawson, Milton Keynes.

"Absolutely fantastic. Makes us proud to reside in Leeds. A reminder of how dynamic we are!!"
The Tidman Family, Farsley.

"Unbelievable amount of work and thought in each panel, with superb results."
Peter Appleton, Stafford.

"Highly imaginative, creative and inspirational. A tactile time capsule."
Rachel Blain, Leeds 6.

"Like nothing I've ever seen before. Superb!"
Darren Fawcett, Leeds.

"This is a truly magnificent work and should have a permanent home in Leeds for all to view it."
Christine Wood, Leeds 17

Every one of the volunteers and all the sponsors can feel proud of the contribution they made. There is now no doubt that we did something worthwhile and that the Tapestry will continue for many years to bring delight to the senses, move the heart and revive the soul.

Acknowledgements

By acknowledging any individual there is always a danger that others who made substantial contributions may have been excluded. Nevertheless the authors wish to thank the following people and organisations without whom the Tapestry would not yet have been completed:

The Earl and Countess of Harewood
The National Lottery through the Arts Council of England
The Trustees of the Peter Moores Foundation

Anonymous Donor	E J Arnold Trust	Renee Silverman
Barclays Bank plc	Evans of Leeds plc	Shirley Gale
Betty Bertrand	Merel Jackson	Sylvia Crowther

There are a handful of people without whom this book would not have appeared so soon after the end of the project. Many thanks to Olav Arnold, Heather Dixon, Audrey Gabbitas, Kevin Goodrum of Printsource, Brian Peace, Renee Silverman and Roger Watkins.

Contents

The Tapestry Panels

Civic Pride

1. University of Leeds
Eileen Wilson (12hrs)

2. Leeds Federation TG
Jean Atkinson

3. The Queen's Hotel
Caroline Dunn (5hrs)

4. White Rose Lacemakers
Marie Kell

5. Inner Wheel
Eileen Wilson

6. Rotary International
Marian C Jenner (6hrs)

7. Smith Devenish
Eileen Wilson (12hrs)

8. FSB Leeds Branch
Eileen Wilson

9. Wigton MoorSchool
Bridget Beer & Mary Needleman
William Beer, Jennifer Barber
Mark & Hannah

10. The Forrests
Eileen Wilson (40hrs)

11. Leeds Care Homes
Myra Turner (9hrs)

12. Women in Management
Catherine Lee (36hrs)

13. The Midland Bank
Janet Grainger (4hrs)

14. Yearly Accountancy
Joyce James (7hrs)

15. Oriental Academy
Eileen Wilson

16. Lex
Judith Gambol

17. Foxwood Mount
Avril Bellwood

18. NHS Executive
Lesley Dove (5hrs)

19. Luncheon Club
Audrey Pidgeon (20hrs)

20. Society for Single Women
Lesley Dove (40hrs)

21. Ashfield Nursing Home
Audrey Pidgeon (6hrs)

22. Lawnswood Dental Care
Joyce James

23. Leeds Civic Trust

24. Leeds Grammar School

25. Civic Hall
Edith Vertigan

26. Cllr Keith Loudon 93/94
Beverley Silverman

27. Cllr Christina Myers 94/95
Beverley Silverman

28. Cllr Peggy White 95/96
Beverley Silverman

29. Cllr Malcolm Bedford 96/97
Beverley Silverman

30. Mandela Gardens
Gill Cook & Jan Webster

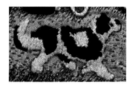

31. Dog
Val Gomersall

32. Dog
Val Gomersall

33. Two Girls

34. Girl with pom-poms

35. Crowd
Mary Mawson

36. Sue Braithwaite and
family by Sue (18hrs)

37. Lord Mayor's Party
Freda Copley (30hrs)

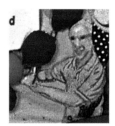

38. George Wildman
Claire Wildman

39. Crowd
Claire Wildman

40.Crowd

41. Crowd
Judith Gambol

42. Crowd
Joyce James

43. Crowd

44. Children (Jill's son)
Jill Rutter (12hrs)

45. Crowd
Ann McL Dabbs

46. Crowd
Barbara Gray

47. Small Girl in Red
Val Gomersall

48. Leeds Fans
Barbara Gray

49. Two on Steps
Denise Teed

50. Crowd

51. The Dunns
Ena Dunn

52 Jarvis Parkway Hotel & Country Club
Myra Turner (12hrs)

53. Bryan & Co
Syvia Tancock (1hr)

54.OPP 2K
Margaret Clark (3hrs)

55. Barclays Bank

56. Toulston Polo Club
Eileen Wilson

57. Kenneth Rutter Ltd
Jill Rutter

58. JCS Auto Refinishers

59. Leeds Church Institute
Sylvia Tancock (2hrs)

60. Church of England
Joyce James

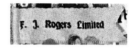

61. FJ Rogers Ltd
Margaret Kingston (3hrs)

62. Parade Organisers
Eileen Wilson (7hrs)

63. F Drake & Co of Golcar
Barbara Town (6hrs)

64. Jarvis Porter Group plc
Myra Turner

65. Victoria Quarter

66. Marks & Spencer
Angela Turner (28hrs)

67. WT Partnership
Merel Jackson (6hrs)

68. Barlow Refactory Products

69. Willmott Dixon
Eileen Wilson

70. Cranswick Watson
Joyce James

71. The Burton Group plc
Joyce James

72. Haley's Restaurant
Joyce James

t73. Airedale
Airconditioning
Syvia Tancock (2.5hrs)

74. Leeds TEC
Eileen Wilson (12hrs)

75. Leeds Girls' High School
Eileen Wilson (11.5hrs)

76. Electromec Access
Joyce James

77. St Gemma's Hospice
Betty Hoggart

78. The National Trust
Joyce James

79. Headingley Hall
Audrey Pidgeon (6hrs)

80. Network
Joan Holah

81. The Whitkirk, Sports and Social Club
Barbara Gray (6hrs)

82. The Yarn Shop
Eileen Wilson (5hrs)

83. MKC Sewing Machines
Joyce James

84. Gosnay's Sports Agency
Jan Oddy

85. Leeds Metropolitan
Joyce James

86. Northern Lights
Lesley Dove

87. Parton Products
Eileen Wilson (5hrs)

88. HE & FJ Brown
Merel Jackson

89. The Merrion
Judith Reynolds

90. Friends of Leeds Museums
Joyce James

91. Leeds Mencap
Joyce James

92. Solk Furniture
Eileen Wilson (7hrs)

93. Metanoics
Mary Cook

94. Co Ventures
Gina Day (40hrs)

95. Crowd
Ann Cove

96. Age Concern
Maureen Spearing (2.5hrs)

97. Weetwood Hall
Avril Bellwood

98. Road Cycling Club
Rita Dobson (20hrs)

99. Crowd

100. Armley Mills Museum
Joan Holah (10hrs)

101. Guide Flag
Gina Day

102. David Kelly Cars

103. Crowd

104. Man

105. Parton Producs
Sheila Haughton (6hrs)

106. Crowd
Val Gomersall +

107. Girl on Bike
Mary Mawson

108. Man in Wheelchair
Kathy Schofield

109. Lorry
Sarah Hodgson

110. Man with Flag
Enid Gator (20hrs)

111. Two People

112. Two People
Denise Teed

113. Crowd

114. Small Person
Textile Art Group

115. Three People
Denise Teed

116. Two People
Barbara Walker

117. Small Person
Dorothy Wrench

118. Two on steps
TAG

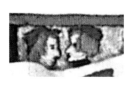

119. Two People
Freda Copley

120. Person in Blue

124. Women in Design & Construction
Joyce James

121. Football Fans
Barbara Gray

122. Two Youths

123. Three Youths
Ann Cove

125. Two People
Barbara Walker

126. Three Children
Freda Copley

127. One Lady
Dorothy Wrench

128. Girls' High Pupil
Jill Rothwell

129. Jill's Daughter
Jill Rutter

130. Wigton Moor Pupils
Bridget Beer & Mary Needleman

131. Lady with Flag
Gillian Kempner

132. Crowd
Margaret Clark

133. Man Waving
Freda Copley

134. Girl Waving
Freda Copley

135. Englafot
Audrey Pidgeon

136. Small Crowd Waving
Freda Copley (4hrs)

137. Small Girl
Freda Copley (4hrs)

138. Two People
Freda Copley

139. Crowd

140. Crowd

141. Crowd
Barbara Gray

142. Man
Denise Teed

143. Two People
Freda Copley

144. Crowd

145. Small Round Person

146. Two Veiled Women

147. Small Person

148. Girl with Black Hair

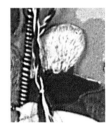

149. Grey-haired Lady
Anna McL Dabbs

150. Lady in Sari

151. Red-haired Boy

152. Lady with Daughter
Dorothy Wrench

153. Two Children

154.Jim Stephenson
Ann Brown (8.5hrs)

155. Jester
Beverley Silverman

156. Couple
Gillian Holding

157. Crowd of Children
Janet Carding

158. Children with Football
Dorothy Wrench

159. Lady near Flowers
Freda Copley

160. Flower Basket
Freda Copley

161. Cameraman
Betty Bertrand

162. Man leading Horses
Ann Francis & F Copley

163. Policewoman

164. Lady with Camera
Kathy Schofield

165. Englafot Lorry
Gina Day

6.
Rotary International
Marian C Jenner

Sample
Edith Vertigan (192hrs)

As a result of the experiences of attempting to involve local businesses on the Enterprise Panel, Kate realised that for many small businesses £500 minimum sponsorship was just too much even though some would have liked to have been involved. Kate said "The Lord Mayor's Parade seemed to be a perfect event in which to involve them. It would represent a civic occasion at the end of the millennium and have room to incorporate the flags of many organisations without losing the integrity of the design. The idea was very popular and although it again took longer than we thought, we had little problem in 'selling' the smaller flags."

This, the fourth panel to be made, not only involved more sponsors but also more volunteers. Many of those who were still embroidering at the end will mention their first piece being done for this panel.

"I called in to see what was happening in Armley Mills and met Kate in the work room. I was hesitant about stitching a piece, but Kate offered me a flag (54) which was quite small. It was a week before I dared thread a needle and start sewing" Margaret Clark, Volunteer

The launch of this panel was at one of the many lunches at the Queen's Hotel and flags were 'sold' and pinned to the cartoon of the panel in the space preferred by each sponsor. To get the necessary viewpoint of the Civic Hall and Mandela Gardens which would give the most visually credible space to the crowds, Kate had to get permission from various bodies to take photos from the upper storeys of their buildings along the Great George Street edge of the gardens. Photographs of the 1995 Lord Mayor's

Parade were also used, some loaned by the Lord Mayor's Office and Mickey Roo (Leeds City Council Planning Dept) and others, concentrating more on the crowds, were taken by Paul Wilkinson and Kate.

As so often happened during the course of the project , fund raising, event organising, consultation, administration and research became so time consuming that Kate had little time to do what she loved most, the drawing and embroidery. Fortunately Sue Hodgson's husband Trevor, who like Sue and Kate was a trained illustrator, was persuaded by his wife to draw up the full scale cartoon from the collage of sketches, postcards, photographs and photocopies gathered by Kate. In common with all of the other panels the number of sponsored pieces changed throughout the planning and working of Civic Pride, and even at the eleventh hour more clubs, schools and small businesses were being added to the piece. Fortunately throughout it all the Civic Hall and Mandela Gardens remained a constant. These were two of

Kate stitching pieces to the panel.

107.
Girl on Bike
Mary Mawson

the most time-consuming pieces in the whole project and realising this they were both started before the completion of the cartoon. Edith Vertigan took on the Civic Hall, and after much discussion with Kate they were both so determined that the building would not just consist of solid blocks of colour that Edith did a sample piece almost as big as the final work. She studied the Civic Hall at various times of day, in different weathers picking out the greens, mauves, pinks, yellows, greys and ivories which create the effect of light glancing off the Portland stone and giving life to the building. The preparatory work was not wasted, not only did it lead to the stunning representation on the skyline of this panel but it has also been used throughout the project to inspire and enlist new volunteers at exhibitions, displays and talks. Edith patiently spent 2,271 hours on the Civic Hall piece and in days when the Tapestry was at Armley Mills she was often to be seen sitting at the

window involved in the general chat but letting the various workshops go on around her while she completed her mammoth task.

The Mandela Garden project was worked from a detailed photograph of the flower displays there in 1995, by two members of the Embroiderers' Guild, Gill Cook and Jan Webster. The original embroidery worked in machine and hand stitching was delivered in good time to the workshop at Armley Mills Museum, presented on card and carefully wrapped up. Such pieces of embroidery were at this stage pinned to the developing full scale cartoon and covered in transparent polythene, so that visitors to the Museum, as well as the volunteers, could see the full colour, three dimensional 'jigsaw' of the panel growing week by week. Hopefully this would inspire others to join the group or put forward their ideas or get to work with renewed enthusiasm on the piece they had at home.

Tragically this and another piece, both exquisitely worked, disappeared from the workshop. The other piece was a portrait of the backs of figures by Beverley Silverman. Telephoning the volunteers at home to confess the loss was one of the most difficult things Kate had to do during the entire project. "How could I tell them what had happened to their labours of love whilst they were in my care?" She could hardly believe it when, in spite of being upset and possibly angry, both Jan and Gill agreed to redo the gardens piece and this at a time when both were having some personal problems. Beverley also forgave Kate and continued to work on the four miniature portraits of the Lord Mayors who were in office during the years the panel was being designed

116.
Two People
Barbara Walker

25.
Civic Hall
Edith Vertigan

Crowd
Anne Cove

166.
Running Dog
Val Gomersall

28.
Cllr Peggy White
Beverley Silverman

110.
Man with Flag
Enid Gator

The spirit of generosity and love of needlework shown by these three artists typifies the warmth, enthusiasm, courage and determination which not only made the project possible but kept Kate going during the bleakest times.

Although many embroiderers who have figures on this panel, including Beverley, Jan, Gill, Freda Copley, Anne Cove, Ann Brown, Sue and Sarah Hodgson, Gillian Holding, Mary Mawson and Denise Teed all have drawing experience and were bold enough to attempt likenesses, the vast majority of volunteers really dreaded tackling faces. It was difficult therefore to persuade people to take the figure projects, unless they were given back views! Even though many avoided faces there were some very inventive 'hairdos', fur and unspun wool and in the case of the lady on the bike (107) Mary went to her hairdresser, asked for the samples on the colour chart and was given cuttings from her stylists own hair.

All manner of strategies and techniques were employed to encourage people to 'have a go', including Denise Teed's transfer painting workshops and DIY sheets and having others - usually Kate or Ann Brown -

draw/paint the faces. Other strategies included pairing hesitant volunteers with more confident ones and holding 'skill sharing' days where a number of people would show their ways of tackling the problem.

Although using a commercial printer to transfer photographic images onto fabric was by this time a well established process for us - and used to great effect on the Civic Hall piece (16 sections carefully heat pressed onto canvas) - it was very costly. The discovery that we could do this ourselves was not made in time to be used for figures on this panel. Ann Brown's portrait of Jim Stephenson (154) holding the Queen's Banner was actually recognised by a member of his family during a very brief showing of the Civic Pride panel on TV after the panel's unveiling. We were all delighted at this successful outcome as Jim, then Manager of the Queen's, had been so enormously supportive of the project in the early years. Most people on this panel are imaginary though there are a few real people. Ena Dunn embroidered herself and her husband (51) and Claire Wildman did a portrait of her late husband. When he retired he was presented with artists paints which he used when he joined a girl's sixth form to study for Art A level. After he died Claire used the paints for his portrait (38) for this panel.

Many workshops and DIY sheets were offered to volunteers to create balloons of all shapes and sizes, the balloon motif being a very useful one for filling in the odd awkward corner or adding colour where necessary. The repeated rhythms of heads, balloons and flags, carefully constructed to embody movement would, Kate hoped, give the desired effect of a merry jostling crowd. The people who made balloons have not been listed, but the quest to find them all is not over. So far Sarah Hodgson, Renee Silverman, Rosemary Cysarz , Betty Bertrand , Barbara Kitchen, Jeanne Sinister and Jean Atkinson have come forward.

This panel was one of the toughest to collate; even though Freda Copley made the process easier by stitching the narrow crowd sections at each side of the Civic Hall on to a separate piece of cloth which was then attached to the backcloth. The whole of the Civic Hall canvas had to be 'quilted' in sections to the backing fabric so the two fabrics would become one. The same process was followed with the Mandela Gardens and then every balloon, person and flag had to be carefully stitched. Cries of "not another flag, balloon or tassel" still ring in the ears. When the 'fine tuning' stage was reached, embellishing the sky with nets, beads and sequins and painting shadows, it was a great relief.

When the first 15 panels were complete and on display, all together for the first time, at Harewood House in 2002, the Deputy Lord Mayor, Cllr Michael Fox, invited all of the volunteers to a Civic reception in, and a tour of the Civic Hall. It was constructed in the 1930's to give gainful employment to the unemployed.

81.
The Whitkirk, Sports and Social Club
Barbara Gray

Sir John Savile (1556-1630), the first Alderman of Leeds was honoured with the three silver owls from his family crest being used in the town's coat of arms, coupled with the fleece as a symbol of the staple trade. When Charles II granted the town a fresh charter in 1661 and Thomas Danby was appointed Mayor the black band with three silver stars from his personal arms were added to the crest. *Pro Rege et Lege* (for King and Law) was added in 1836 following the reconstitution of the corporation and finally in 1921, the owls were changed to brown, a golden helmet added and the whole recorded at the College of Arms. The owls now stand as a symbol of the City of Leeds and Kate thought it appropriate to include at least one on each panel. Now that the panels are all on display 'counting the owls' has become a popular pastime with the public and at its first exhibition at Harewood a competition was held with a prize for the correct number counted.

The Tapestry was to represent a glimpse in time near the millennium, knowing that much of the cityscape would change in the future. Often we resent permanent features disappearing from our landscape but in the case of Mandela Gardens, despite its beauty, perhaps it had lost its significance when Nelson Mandela was freed.

130.
Wigton Moor Pupils
Bridget Beer & Mary Needleman and pupils.

121.
Football Fans
Barbara Gray

Local Faces

1. Market Roofs
Joyce James (25hrs)

2. Car Park
Joyce James (10hrs)

3. Roofs
Joyce James (28hrs)

4.Building
Merel Jackson

5. Eye Clinic
Pauline Clayden

6. Building
Myra Turner (14hrs)

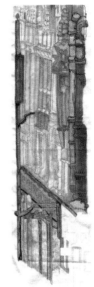

7. Waterstones
Gill Cook

8. Building tops
Betty Bertrand

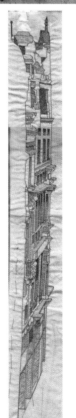

9. Building
Janet Taylor

10. Senza Building
Eileen Wilson

11/12. Albion Street
Ruth Fowler, Lynne Ward &
Diane Allott

13. River Island
Sally Walton (40hrs)

14. Longley Building
Clare Bryan

15. Doctor Hey
Ann Brown (50hrs)

16. Doctor Hook
Barbara Gray

17. James Watt
Denise Teed (7hrs)

18. Joseph Priestley
Denise Teed (8hrs)

19. John Barran MP
Denise Teed

20. Ralph Thoresby
Denise Teed (50hrs)

21. Thoresby's Plinth
Denise Teed (2hrs)

22. Phil May
Ann Brown (20hrs)

23. Leeds Phil & Lit
Brenda Archer

24.P.M.Asquith
Ena Dunn (20hrs)

25. The Thoresby Society
Eileen Wilson (30hrs)

26. Leonora Cohen
Karen Pattison (5hrs)

27. John Harrison
Betty Bertrand

28. Chair, Table etc
Denise Teed (6hrs)

29. Table Tops
Betty Bertrand

30.Cuthbert Broderick
Jackie Ryder

31. Alice Bacon
Joan Gamble

32. Ellen Heaton
Janet Taylor

33. Suffragettes
B Gray & J Holah

34. Mr & Mrs Mees
Pauline Clayden (18hrs)

35. Rev. Don Robbins
Janet Taylor

36. John Smeaton
Janet Taylor (4hrs)

37. Mr & Mrs Mackintosh
Eileen Wilson (100hrs)

38. Votes for Women
James Joyce

39. Ivy Benson
Betty Bertrand

40. Rev. Jenkinson
Merel Jackson

41. Woodbine Willie
Ena Dunn (20hrs)

42. Caryl Phillips
Janet Taylor

43. "Katy"
Clare Bryan & Janet Taylor

44. Mr & Mrs Hodgson
Joan Holah

45. Diana Rigg
Gillian Holding

46. Jeremy Paxman
Myra Turner (3.5hrs)

47. Griselda Pollock
Janet Taylor

48. Jack Higgins
Betty Bertrand

49. Jude Kelly
Ann Brown (36hrs)

50. Frankie Vaughan
Anne Cove

51. John Battle
Sheila Eagleton (32hrs)

52. Councillor Minkin
Jackie Ford

53. Peter O'Toole
Freda Copley

54. Kay Mellor
Jackie Ford

55. Denis Healey
Renee Silverman (50hrs)

56. Sylvia & Her Mum
Sallie Lindley (25hrs)

57. Nadine Senior
Jackie Ford

58. Willis Hall
Val Gomersall (6.5hrs)

59.Gael Lindenfield
Janet Taylor

60. Keith Waterhouse
Janet Taylor

61. Char March
Janet Taylor

62. James Brown
Margaret Booth

63. Barbara Taylor Bradford
A Brown & J Taylor

64. Liz Dawn
Janet Taylor

65. Bernard Atha
Janet Taylor

66. Claire Frisby
Janet Taylor

67. Christa Ackroyd
Janet Taylor

68. Susan Pitter
Janet Taylor (6hrs)

69. Sue Reddington
Val Gomersall (26hrs)

70.Bill Killgallon
Eileen Gibb

71. Doreen Newlyn
Barbara Gray (34hrs)

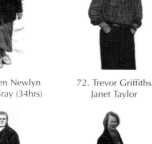
72. Trevor Griffiths
Janet Taylor

77. Jimmy Savile
Denise Teed

73. Mel B
Janet Taylor

74. Susan Marsden
Ann Brown (43hrs)

75. Tony Harrison
Ann Brown

76. Mrs Phyllis Pask

78. Book
Joan Holah (4.5hrs)

79. SJR by Barbara Gray
80. McCourt Newton Ltd by
Margaret Clark

81. Owl
Joyce James

82. One Stop Architects
Gwen Woolliscroft

83. Vilene
Joyce James

84. Rhubarb the Cat
Renee Silverman

85. Thoresby Society Crest
Eileen Wilson (60hrs)

86. Englafot by Maureen
Elvidge
87. Yorkshire Chemicals by
Joan Holah (3hrs)

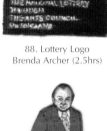

88. Lottery Logo
Brenda Archer (2.5hrs)

89. Samuel Smiles
Brenda Archer (2hrs)

90. Brian Close & Fred
Trueman
Valerie Horner

91. Richard Whiteley
Ann Brown (40hrs)

92. Flt Sgt Aaron
Merel Jackson (25hrs)

93. Jack Johnson
Ann Brown (17hrs)

94. Liz Dawn
Denise Teed

95. Joe Haigh
Gill Cook

96. Sylvia Wright
Ann Brown (52hrs)

97. Maxwell Roberts
Betty Bertrand (24hrs)

98. The Earl of Harewood
Janet Taylor (7hrs)

99. The Countess of Harewood
Janet Taylor

100. Monseigneur Maguire
Janet Carding (12hrs)

101. Lord Merlyn Rees
Janet Taylor (6hrs)

102. Keith Bowen
Mary Sanders

103. Alan Bennett
Beverley Silverman

104. Mary Sheepshanks
Janet Taylor

105. Fanny Waterman
Beverley Silverman

106. Richard Hoggart
Janet Taylor (4hrs)

Local Faces

90.
Brian Close
& Fred Trueman
Valerie Horner

91.
Richard Whiteley
Ann Brown (40hrs)

77.
Jimmy Savile
Denise Teed

45.
Diana Rigg
Gillian Holding

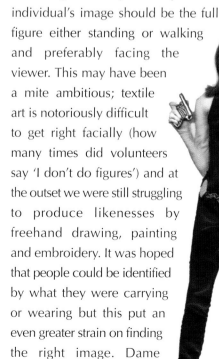

Research, and looking for nominations for the Local Faces panel, began in 1995 and it was yet another subject for which it was difficult to find sponsorship. Many of the potential participants had been dead for at least a hundred years, which was something of a disadvantage, and it did not seem entirely appropriate to ask those still with us to pay to be honoured in this way. However, it must be said that many of those nominated did give a generous donation when they appreciated the funding difficulties.

Initially there were to be about sixty people represented on the panel from both public life and those less well-known who have made a contribution to Leeds. It was hoped to have an equal balance of men and women and 'positive discrimination' was employed to portray the rich ethnic diversity of the city. As with other panels, despite requests through the media, volunteer newsletters and word of mouth, nominations were slow in coming. There was slightly more success when the full-scale cartoon of the panel beautifully drawn by Anne Croft, was displayed at two of the fund-raising lunches.

The Yorkshire Post were reluctant to help in the quest to find who the public wanted on the panel, so Willis Hall and Keith Waterhouse were invited to one of the lunches at the Queen's Hotel, along with Kay Mellor to help raise the profile in the media. It was upsetting after this to read in the press that Willis Hall thought that half a day in the public library would identify the appropriate people. The spirit of the Tapestry has always been to involve the public and listen to their choices about what should be represented on each of the panels. When people had been nominated the next job was to set about finding suitable images to

choose from, if indeed there were any to be found. Research volunteers spent nearly a year sifting through magazines, newspapers and books in the archive department of the Yorkshire Post and at the City Library with the help of librarian Sue Cook.

Ann Wheatley and six other volunteers then formed a team to sift through the nominations finally received. Flt Sgt Arthur Louis Aaron VC was the most popular choice to be represented with Dennis Healey, Phyllis Pask, Danny Freeman, PM Asquith, Brian Close and Gael Lindenfield also being very popular. Some nominations were for relatively unknown people and it was part of the team's task to find out whether they merited inclusion. Several failed to get onto the panel because images of them have still not been found. Mary Seacole (a heroine of the stature of Florence Nightingale) and Dr Ashoke Bannerjea (first black magistrate in Leeds) fall into this category.

The design of the panel required that the individual's image should be the full figure either standing or walking and preferably facing the viewer. This may have been a mite ambitious; textile art is notoriously difficult to get right facially (how many times did volunteers say 'I don't do figures') and at the outset we were still struggling to produce likenesses by freehand drawing, painting and embroidery. It was hoped that people could be identified by what they were carrying or wearing but this put an even greater strain on finding the right image. Dame

Diana Rigg was to be portrayed in her most popular incarnation as Emma Peel from *The Avengers*. It seems unbelievable now that it took eighteen months to find a suitable picture. Dame Diana herself was co-opted to the task when she was appearing as Phaedre at the Albery Theatre in London. Even she only managed to find a much photocopied image in a small black and white leaflet. Fortunately the Tapestry researchers are tenacious and finally Julia Cooper found just the right photograph in a book on stars of the silver screen in a comic collector's shop. Though the actress herself would have preferred to have been represented in one of her more serious roles, she accepts this is how people like to see her.

Some of the others chosen for the panel also lent themselves to being identified by their accoutrements. Brian Close and Fred Trueman are unmistakable in their beautifully knitted pullovers and it could only be Frankie Vaughan with black suit and cane doing the high kick. He delighted the guests at a Tapestry lunch with his impromptu rendition of 'Gimme the Moonlight'. Anne Cove, who embroidered this piece, had to get her son David to model the high kick for her drawing and later pose in a double breasted jacket for further sketches.

Sir Jimmy Savile, Peter O'Toole as Lawrence of Arabia and Richard Whiteley are also easily identifiable, but with other, perhaps less visually well-known people, it was a relief when photographic techniques could be used. This also gave greater confidence to many of the embroiderers and led to joining several photographs together to make a more suitable image. Liz Johnson, one of the researchers, wrote to Jeremy Paxman asking for a photograph of himself with the usual requirements for the panel (full length, looking ahead, preferably in colour etc). He sent a good image of just his head and shoulders. When she approached him again for permission to add another body he replied that, given the choice, he would like Arnold Swarzenegger's. The volunteers took him up on this and with the aid of an early book of Swarzenegger's body building the two were grafted together. The result was a muscular body with the smiling face of the 'thinking woman's crumpet' at a rakish angle. Though amused, Mr Paxman preferred to be represented in a more dignified manner and yet again limbs, torso and suit were borrowed from a member of Barbara's family.

50.
Frankie Vaughan
Anne Cove

The nominations process was officially open for six years. The required number of people had been reached, the design had been finalised and embroidered figures were being stitched to the backcloth and still a few more people crept onto the panel. Councillor Bernard Atha for instance, in 1992 felt the project was far too ambitious to get off the ground but he is now one of the project's most vocal supporters so the Trustees were delighted to include him. During his year as Lord Mayor he attended several Tapestry events and made a memorable speech during the unveiling of the Pins and Needles Panel. When he became Lord Mayor he said that he would like to highlight the great contribution that women have made to the success of the city and that he would be calling on like women of all degrees to act as Lady Mayoress throughout the year. Four of them are shown on the panel with Bernard.

53.
Peter O'Toole
Freda Copley

84.
Rhubarb the Cat
Renee Silverman

92.
Flt. Sgt. Aaron
Merel Jackson (25hrs)

Rhubarb the cat (84) was also a last-minute addition. There had been a search for a heroic pet for many years, through radio, press and volunteer newsletters, but to no avail. Sylvia, our fundraiser finally brought in a photograph of her mother-in-law's cat and her feline credentials to appear on the panel. Mrs Crowther had gone to bed without putting the guard round her coal fire. Rhubarb slept beside the fire, and during the night a hot coal had jumped from the fire and started smouldering on the hearth rug. The cat had then gone upstairs and woken her mistress by scratching at her face, thus avoiding a very serious fire. As a reward for this heroic deed Rhubarb's weekly treat of crab increased to twice a week and for the rest of her life she slept on her owner's old beaverskin coat. Unfortunately the photograph of this special cat was too small and unclear, but after searching magazines, greeting cards and the internet Renee Silverman managed to perform the necessary surgical operation, using Photoshop, to immortalise Rhubarb's memory.

During the nominations process the full-scale cartoon of the panel, beautifully illustrated by Anne Croft, was shown at many venues including Harewood House in 1999 when all panels, some finished and some in the planning stage were shown together for the first time. Many of the figures represented were from the first stage of research and were there to give an overall impression of the finished design before their credentials for connection with Leeds had been properly checked. Alma Cogan, Helen Shapiro, Brian Glover and Brian Blessed fell into this category. Despite the rigorous research

one person appears on the panel who has no connection with Leeds. Four hundred years ago and more there were two *worthies* with the name John Harrison, one a Leeds man and the other from Hull. Both were nominated in press coverage of the great and the good of Yorkshire during the Millennium celebrations and the image of John Harrison of Hull has managed to settle himself at a table with the people of Leeds! Our own John has not been forgotten though. He appears on the *Faith in Leeds* panel next to the church he was responsible for building.

One of the advantages of producing a cartoon of the panel is that criticism can be taken on board before it is too late and can often draw others into getting involved with this community project. Councillor Graham Latty of Aireborough Ward received a written complaint from a constituent to the effect that the uniform in our drawing of Arthur Louis Aaron was incorrect. He contacted the Tapestry asking if this could be rectified and also confessed that despite the fact that the project was into its seventh year he had not heard about it. By this time the full research had been done by Brian Jackson from the 'selection team' and the embroidery of Aaron, in correct uniform, had been finished but Councillor Latty's interest had been awakened. He was told how the project was neither initiated, nor financially supported, by Leeds City Council and was invited to the next unveiling event. He came, he saw, he admired and in due course joined the Board of Trustees where he made many valuable contributions over the next few years. This is just one example where criticism can be positive, but all too often the *British Reserve* gets in the way of critics identifying themselves thus preventing a satisfactory dialogue between the two parties.

Physically the panel came together very well with Merel and Shirley doing the lion's share of the stitching.

When this panel was first contemplated, Kate visualised people promenading down one of Leeds most beautiful streets. Albion Place, with the Longley Building clad in Burmantoft tiles, the Senza building with its elegant windows and the domes of Kirkgate Market in the distance seemed to be an interesting and stately background to honour the great and the good of Leeds.

The biographies of those included on the panel are necessarily brief. Many of them warrant a book in their own right, but these short notes should give a flavour of the many reasons for their inclusion.

Dr Hook (1798-1875) became Vicar of Leeds in 1837 and reorganised the parishes of Leeds. He was responsible for the building of 21 churches, including a new Parish Church and 30 new schools. As early as 1846 he was trying to establish education for all children through rate-paid schools.

James Watt (1736-1819) was not the first choice to be in City Square but Councillor Wainwright felt he should be there and offered to pay for the bronze statue. His engines powered many of the factories of Leeds, but fewer than Matthew Murray's and it is rumoured that he actually bought the land around Murray's engineering works to prevent his expansion.

Joseph Priestley was born in Birstall in 1733, became a clergyman at the age of 22, Minister of Mill Hill Chapel (1767-73), the founder of Leeds Library, a scientist most famous for his discovery of oxygen.

Radolphus Thoresby (1658-1725) kept a diary for nearly 30 years and wrote the first published history of Leeds *Ducatus Leodiensis*. His should have been the fourth statue in the square though perhaps the Thoresby Society founded in 1889 is a more fitting tribute to an early local historian.

Doctor Hey (1736-1819) was a founder of Leeds Infirmary where he worked as a surgeon for 45 years. He gave anatomy lessons using the bodies of criminals executed at York, including the body of Mary Bateman, whose dissection became a side show.

John Barran MP (1821-1905) was the first to produce ready-made mass-produced clothing with the aid of the Greenwood and Batley band-knife (for cutting several layers of cloth at a go) and the Singer sewing machine. The Moorish building in Park Square was originally his warehouse.

Phil May (1864-1903) was born in Leeds. He was a cartoonist for *Punch* from 1895 and also issued his own *Phil May's Winter Annual*.

A Asquith, PM (1852-1928) was born in Morley. He was Liberal Prime Minister from 1908 to 1916 and was responsible

1.
Market Roofs
Joyce James (25hrs)

3.
Roofs
Joyce James (25hrs)

15.
Doctor Hey
Ann Brown (50hrs)

18.
Joseph Priestley
Denise Teed (8hrs)

11/12 Albion Street
Ruth Fowler, Lynne Ward & Diane Allott

26.
Leonora Cohen
Karen Pattison (5hrs)

40.
Rev. Jenkinson
Merel Jackson

30.
Cuthbert Broderick
Jackie Ryder

42.
Caryl Phillips
Janet Taylor

44.
Mr & Mrs Hodgson
Joan Holah

for introducing the Old Age Pension and Conscription.

Leonora Cohen OBE (1873-1978) was a suffragette imprisoned for her political beliefs. She became first woman president of the Leeds Trades Council in 1923 and was a magistrate.

John Harrison (1693-1776) was born in Foulby near Hull. He invented the marine chronometer in 1761 which determined longitude within 18 geographical miles - a much smaller margin of error than we have here!

Cuthbert Broderick was born in 1821 in Hull. He trained as an architect and won competitions to design the Town Hall, Corn Exchange and Mechanic's Institute.

Alice Bacon (1910-93) was born in Normanton. She trained as a teacher and became the first female MP for Leeds (Labour) in 1945. She became Baroness Bacon of Leeds and Normanton in 1970.

Ellen Heaton (1816-94) was an influential pre-Raphaelite art patron and an active campaigner for women's rights, education, environment issues and against vivisection. She was also a friend of Rossetti, the Brownings and Ruskin. She lived in Clarendon Square.

Mr & Mrs Riches were sponsored by their sons.

Rev Don Robbins was Vicar of St George's Church from 1930-45. As a direct response to the suffering during the Depression he cleared out the crypt of the Church to provide a rest room for the men. Over the years this has expanded to provide food, shelter and advice for anyone who needs it.

John Smeaton (1724-94) attended Leeds Grammar School and went on to be known as the father of Civil Engineering, working on such projects as the third Eddystone Lighthouse, the Calder Navigation and the

Clyde Canals. He founded the Society of Civil Engineers in 1771.

Charles and Marion Mackintosh were sponsored by their two daughters.

Ivy Benson (1913-1993) was born in Holbeck. Ivy was leader of an all girl band *Ivy Benson and her Rhythm Girl Band.* The band survived for over forty years and when the Sex Discrimination Act came in, in 1975, she happily interviewed men for inclusion stipulating that they had to be prepared to fit into a dress sized 10-16!

Rev. Jenkinson, the socialist vicar of Holbeck in 1927, helped to produce a report on slum clearance and a programme of building 30,000 new houses including the controversial Quarry Hill Flats.

Woodbine Willie (1883-1929) was a Church of England Minister and poet. He was awarded the Military Cross in 1917 for his work in the First World War. His nickname comes from his habit of comforting the weary troops with cigarettes 'For the men to whom I owed God's Peace/I put off with a cigarette'.

Caryl Phillips was born 1958 in St Kitts and moved to Leeds when he was three months old. He won a place at Oxford in 1976 to read English and now writes plays and novels including *Strange Fruit* and *Final Passage.*

Katy is based on a character by Leeds based cartoonist Jacky Fleming

Mr & Mrs Hodgson Alice and Raymond were sponsored by their family for Mrs Hodgson's 80th birthday. A surprise for both Mrs Hodgson and the tapestry volunteers at Harewood.

Local Faces

Diana Rigg CBE was born 1938 in Doncaster but spent her teenage years in Leeds. Educated at Fulneck she won an award from Leeds Council to study at RADA and joined the RSC in 1959. She is perhaps best known for her role as Emma Peel in *The Avengers*. Patron of the Tapestry.

Jeremy Paxman was born in Leeds and brought up in Worcestershire. Principally known as the anchor man on *Newsnight*; has also been presenter of *University Challenge* since 1994.

Griselda Pollock was born 1951 in Canada and educated at Oxford. She moved to Leeds in 1977 where she set up the Centre for Cultural Studies at Leeds University.

Jack Higgins was born 1929 in Ireland and came to Leeds aged 9. He left school with no qualifications but has since gained a degree as a mature student, been a teacher and written international best sellers including *The Eagle has Landed*.

Jude Kelly OBE was born 1954 in Liverpool. She is represented on the Tapestry as Artistic Director of the Playhouse.

Frankie Vaughan CBE (1928-99) was born in Liverpool and came to Leeds College of Art where his singing talent emerged doing Al Jolson impressions during rag week. He was a huge chart-topper in the 1950s and continued to maintain his star status until he died. He was a tireless worker for charity, particularly boys' clubs, for which he was awarded the CBE.

John Battle was born in Bradford. He went to Leeds University and became a Pressure Group Campaigner. He is Labour MP for Leeds West having held two ministerial posts since 1997.

Councillor Elizabeth Minkin is Executive Board Member of Leeds City Council responsible for Development, Strategic Planning and Sustainability.

Peter O'Toole was born 1932 in Ireland and brought up in Hunslet. He was awarded Best Actor of the Year in 1959 for his part in Willis Hall's *The Long and the Short and the Tall*. Best known for his part in *Lawrence of Arabia*.

Kay Mellor started her career as an actress and went on to script writing including *Band of Gold* , *Coronation Street* and her most recent series *Fat Friends*. Patron of the Tapestry.

Denis Healey, Baron of Riddlesden was born 1917 in Keighley. He was labour MP for SE Leeds from 1952 to 1955 and E Leeds from 1955-1992. He was made Freeman of the City of Leeds in 1992.

Sylvia Crowther and her mother Anne Cardiss Wright. Sylvia was fund-raiser for the Tapestry project from 1997 to 2002 when the fifteenth panel was completed.

Nadine Senior MBE was Principal of the Northern School of Contemporary Dance in Chapeltown.

Willis Hall (b1929) is a playwright whose works include *The Long and the Short and the Tall* and collaborative works with Keith Waterhouse. He is also a member of the International Brotherhood of Magicians.

Gael Lindenfield is author of *Positive Woman*. She was responsible for the pioneering preventative mental health project Mind Your Self.

Keith Waterhouse was born 1929 in Hunslet. His best known novel is *Billy Liar* though he is better known to some of the

47. Opposite
Griselda Pollock
Janet Taylor

55.
Denis Healey
Renee Siverman (50hrs)

56.
Sylvia & Her Mum
Sallie Lindley (25hrs)

109.
William Shent
Claire Wildman

65.
Bernard Atha
Janet Taylor

63.
Barbara Taylor Bradford
A Brown & J Taylor

75.
Tony Harrison
Ann Brown

embroiderers as the teenage boy who wrote the Youth Club magazine for Mill Hill.

Char March is an award winning poet and playwright.

James Brown was born 1962 in York. He now lives in Leeds where he makes picture maps and since 2001 he has been making a series of paintings entitled *Mental Maps*.

Barbara Taylor Bradford was born in Leeds. Her first job was as a typist at the Yokshire Post (1958). She became a journalist, moved to Fleet Street and started writing novels, including *A Woman of Substance* and *Hold the Dream*. She now lives in the USA.

Councillor Bernard Atha was Lord Mayor of Leeds 2001/2002. He is shown with his Lady Mayoresses Liz Dawn, Claire Frisby, Christa Ackroyd and Susan Pitter

Sue Reddington MBE is Director of Meanwood Urban Valley Farm, an educational resource committed to empowering people in the community.

Bill Killgallon was former Lord Mayor of Leeds, founder and Director of St Anne's Shelter and Housing Action. He is chairperson of Leeds Hospital Trust

Doreen Newlyn initiated and masterminded to its conclusion (1964-70) the campaign to establish a theatre, the Leeds Playhouse, which became the West Yorkshire Playhouse.

Trevor Griffiths is a playwright.

Mel B is one of the *Spice Girls*.

Susan Marsden was campaigner, co-founder and first chair of Eye on the Aire (1988-92) the organisation to clean up the River Aire. She is also active in the *Right to Roam* campaign.

Tony Harrison is a poet, born 1937 in Hunslet and educated at Leeds Grammar School and Leeds University. He has taught at Universities in Nigeria and Czechoslovakia.

Mrs Phyllis Pask had raised £93,000 by 1990 to sponsor 100 guide dogs. Her charitable works included working for the WRVS at St James and Meanwood Hospital.

Sir Jimmy Savile OBE was born 1928 in Leeds. He became one of the Bevan Boys but after a serious accident he turned to being a DJ and used his celebrity to raise money for charities including £10 million for the Spinal Injuries Department at Stoke Mandeville Hospital.

Samuel Smiles (1812-1905) propogated the philosophy that young people should not believe in the patronage of their parents but should make their own careers with equal opportunities for all. His books included *Self-Help, Character* and *Duty*.

Brian Close was born 1931 in Rawdon. He started to play cricket for Yorkshire in 1949 and captained the team from 1963-1970. His debut for England was when he was 18.

Fred Trueman was born 1931 in Stainton, Yorkshire. He made his cricket test debut in 1952.

Richard Whiteley was the first face to be seen on Channel 4. He has celebrated 3000 editions of *Countdown* and 27 years as anchorman for Calendar, Yorkshire TVs news programme. Well known for his sombre clothing!

Flt Sgt Arthur Louis Aaron (1922-43) was born in Gledhow. He joined the Volunteer Reserve in 1941 and was awarded his pilot wings in June 1942. On August 12, 1943 he was Captain and pilot of a Stirling attacking Turin when the plane was damaged. Though wounded he managed to get his crew back to Algeria where he died soon after. A statue of him was unveiled by the last surviving crew member, Malcolm Mitchell on 24 March 2001 at Eastgate Fountain.

Jack Johnson is the accountant for the Leeds Tapestry and active in the Federation of Small Businesses.

Liz Dawn was born in Burmantofts and is well known for her role in *Coronation Street*. She is also a tireless charity worker for breast cancer treatment, children with learning difficulties and various hospitals.

Joe Haigh MBE was the longest-serving newspaper seller for Yorkshire Post Newspapers. He sold the Yorkshire Evening Post for 75 years retiring in 1998 at the age of 87.

Sylvia Wright was born 1938 in Leeds. She was a nurse and nursing lecturer but gave it all up to work with a mobile clinic in Tamil Nadu, India. Her Trust has also built a Health and Education Centre there.

Maxwell Roberts of the Headrow Gallery.

The Earl of Harewood is a cousin of Her Majesty The Queen. He invented Opera North and is President Of Leeds United FC.

The Countess of Harewood is a Board member of the Young Concert Artists Trust and she works with young people at the Royal College of Music through the Peter Moores Foundation.

Monsignor Canon Peter McGuire is Vicar General of the Diocese of Leeds, Dean of the Cathedral Church of St Anne's Leeds and member of the West Yorkshire Ecumenical Council of Leeds Churches Together.

Lord Merlyn Rees was born 1920 in Wales. He became MP for South Leeds in 1963 and from 1987 was chairman of the South Leeds Groundwork Trust.

Keith Bowen: although a quadriplegic after having his neck broken on police duty, he is active as an advocate for people with learning difficulties and works to help other disabled people.

Alan Bennett was born 1934 in Armley. He became well known in *Beyond the Fringe* and recently with his set of television plays *Talking Heads* and film *The Madness of King George*

Mary Sheepshanks is a poet and successful novelist who lives in Leeds. The *New York Times* compared her to Jane Austen.

Fanny Waterman CBE was the inspiration behind the triennial Leeds International Pianoforte Competition, founded in 1961.

Richard Hoggart was born in 1918 in Chapeltown. He was orphaned early in life but with scholarships succeeded in getting a place at University. He has, since then, written and given talks on the importance of literacy and making learning accessible to all.

Richard Oastler (1789-1861) was born in the slum area which was cleared to build Quarry Hill flats. He campaigned against slum conditions and fought to introduce the Ten Hours Act to reduce working hours. He is buried in St Stephen's Churchyard at Kirkstall.

William Shent (d1787) was a barber and peruke maker. He became the first Superintendent Minister of the Leeds Circuit in 1753 but was expelled for drinking. He lost his job and money and ended up in the workhouse but was re-instated into the Methodist Church when Wesley spoke on his behalf at Shent's tribunal in Keighley

Woodbine Lizzie (d1947) was also known as Tramway Liz. She was born Alice Porter in Stanningley and was a well known figure in Leeds. When her marriage broke down (she had six children) she became a tramp and could usually be seen around Whip Yard and Boar Lane. The police often took her to the Bridewell for a good wash.

110.
Woodbine Lizzie
Denise Teed

103.
Alan Bennett
Beverley Silverman

99.
The Countess of Harewood
Janet Taylor

107.
Richard Oastler
Janet Carding

1. View of Leeds
Angela Turner (100hrs)

2. View of Leeds
Barbara Walker (20hrs)

3. 3rd White Cloth Hall
Merel Jackson (11hrs)

4. Mixed Cloth Hall
Janet Taylor

5. Mixed Cloth Hall
Janet Carding (22hrs)

6. Armley Clothiers Banner
Renee Silverman

7. Painters and Stainers
Beryl Smith

8. The Draper's Company
Lesley Dove (55hrs)

9. James Hare Logo
Valerie Horner (45hrs)

10. Fuller's Teasel
M.T. Sanders

11. Benjamin Gott
Betty Laycock (21hrs)

12. Pear's Advert
Joan Holah (40hrs)

13. Burton Montage
Betty Laycock (24hrs)

14. James Hare Book
Elizabeth Thackrah(2hrs)

15. Duttons for Buttons
Vicky Storr

16. Madeira Threads
Ann Kirk (27hrs)

17. Burton's Suit No. 5
Audrey Pidgeon

18. C & A
Vivienne Brown (4.5hrs)

19. C & A Logo
Brenda Archer(6hrs)

20. Sunstreet Printers
Janet Carding

21. Bond's Shop
Joan Holah

22. Mr & Mrs Bond
Joan Holah

23. Marks and Spencer
Joan Holah

24. Edwardian Ladies
Valerie Horner (95hrs)

25. Lunardi's Balloon
Joan Holah

26. Peacock's Advert
Mary Mawson (23hrs)

27. Peacock's Shop
Mary Mawson (106hrs)

28.School of Textiles
Jan Brown (100hrs)

29. Alfred Brown Ltd
Elizabeth Thackrah (7hrs)

30. Howell Blinds
Janet Taylor

31. Elida Faberge
Evi Malm

32. Witts Printers
Godfrey Harland (115hrs)

33. Top Copy
Janet Taylor

34. Recruitment Poster
Mary Sanders (5hrs)

35. Matthew Murray
Janet Carding (18hrs)

36. John Stansfeld
Janet Carding (20hrs)

37. James Hare's
Godfrey Harland (29hrs)

38. Clariant
Joan Holah

39. Cuthbert Broderick
Janet Carding (26hrs)

40. Pack Horse Yard
Eileen Wilson

41. Clayton, Son & Co.
Betty Bertrand

42. Scattergood & Johnson
Joan Holah

46. Elida Faberge
Betty Laycock (6hrs)

43. Elida Faberge
Kate Russell

44. Holbeck Carnival
Joyce Maynard (20hrs)

45. Small Print
Margaret Clark (13hrs)

47. Rail Rates
Brenda Archer (4hrs)

48. Share Certificate
Janet Taylor

49. Packaging
Betty Laycock (7hrs)

50. Garforth Colliery Barge
Joyce Maynard

51. Murray's Engine
Jan Brown (40hrs)

52. Tram
Godfrey Harland

53. Dougall's Tram
Margaret Clark (55hrs)

54. Steam Engine
Edith Vertigan

55. Tram Ticket
Joyce Maynard

56. The Mallard
Eileen Wilson

57. Mousell Brothers
Mary Mawson (30hrs)

58. Hopkin's Fish Fryers
R Silverman, J Ford
J Taylor, K Russell

59. Smeaton's Engine
Anne Boyle

60. Smocking
Janet Taylor

61. Smocking
Joan Langfield

62. Lax & Shaw
Joan Holah (31hrs)

63. Johnson Radley
Betty Bertrand

64. Lax & Shaw
Betty Bertrand

65. Hare's Bookcover
Elizabeth Thackrah

66. Bernina Club
Sheila Udakis

Pins and Needles

TEXTILE AND INDUSTRIAL HERITAGE

The textile and industrial heritage panel is an amalgamation of two original panels. Kate's original design for *Textiles* had a background of decoupage screening, using modern reproductions such as wrapping paper, cards and books as well as using photographs taken by Paul Wilkinson (son of Jackie) of an original screen at Armley Mills. Following this theme the original *Industry* panel was to have a background of engineering drawings and blue prints with historic bus tickets donated by Donald Wilson and his friends. When it was decided that we should stop seeking sponsors for both panels the two panels were brought together. The combined background was visually too 'busy'. This is just one example of the abortive research and design processes common in the production of these panels. Designs were needed to show to prospective sponsors but these were almost impossible to achieve without knowing which firms and individuals were going to become involved. The idea for the final background of lighter fabrics, with domestic and feminine connotations at the top and the heavier fabrics, with a more industrial and masculine feel, at the bottom, did however evolve from the original ideas. The two themes of textiles and engineering work well together as they go hand in hand with the history of Leeds.

1.
View of Leeds
Angela Turner (100hrs)

On this panel the number of non-sponsored sections is roughly equal to the number chosen by sponsors. Some were selected to set the scene of the Industrial Revolution in the Aire Valley, others for setting the historical context and the remainder for aesthetic reasons. At the top are two paintings of Leeds; the first is *Prospect of Leeds from the Knostrop Hill* painted around 1715 and featured in Thoresby's *Ducatus Leodiensis* (1); the second is by Alphonse Douseau and is a view looking north towards Leeds from Rope Hill in the 1840s (2). In just over a hundred years Leeds had changed dramatically with industrial chimneys, pottery kilns and, in the foreground, Middleton Railway carrying coal from the pits to Hunslet. During the same period men were taking to the skies. Vincenzi Lunardi (secretary to the Italian ambassador in London) was Britain's first aeronaut and made one of his celebrated balloon flights in December 1786 from the area of the White Cloth Hall descending forty minutes later at Thorpe Arch (25).

3.
3rd White Cloth Hall
Merel Jackson (11hrs)

7.
Painters and Stainers
Beryl Smith

Cloth, woven at home, was sold twice weekly at an open market in Lower Briggate. In 1711 the first White (undyed) Cloth Hall was built in Kirkgate in response to a similar building being erected in Wakefield which was threatening to take Leeds' trade away. Business was increasing at such a pace that by 1756 a larger Hall had to be built, followed by a third White Cloth Hall 20 years later. The railway sliced through this magnificent third building in the 1860s but the remains

25.
Lunardi's Balloon
Joan Holah

6.
Armley Clothiers Banner
Renee Silverman

5.
Mixed Cloth Hall
Janet Carding (22hrs)

28.
School of Textiles
Jan Brown (100hrs)

24.
Edwardian Ladies
Valerie Horner (95hrs)

still survive behind the Corn Exchange (3). The first Cloth Hall is also still standing, though boarded up and awaiting renovation. The mixed cloth merchants also wanted a hall which was paid for by subscription. Built in 1756-7 at a cost of £5,300, it stood on the site of City Square and Infirmary Street and was the largest building in Leeds in its time (4). The cupola (5) should look familiar. It was removed before demolition in 1890 and used to top the Hotel Metropole. It was appropriate that the research done for these pieces and the four fashionable ladies (24) should be carried out by Emma Lickfield, seconded to us for a short while by Professor Johnson of the University of Leeds Textile Industries Department (28).

Spinning and weaving were carried out at home, but powerful and expensive fulling mills were needed to complete the process. One of the earliest was Armley Mills (6), built next to the river with a constant supply of water power to drive the machinery to felt the cloth. There are records of a mill

standing on the site since the Dissolution, though in the late 18th century and early 19th century it was all but destroyed in a series of fires. The present building dates back to the time when it was owned by Benjamin Gott (11).

Gott was born in Calverley in 1762, the son of a county surveyor of bridges. His father paid for him to be apprenticed to wool merchants Wormald and Fountaine and by 1790 he was head of this firm. Shortly after this he built Bean Ing, the world's first woollen factory. This factory was also burned to the ground, so when he acquired Armley he realised the need for a different type of structure to be made. The new building had cylindrical cast-iron columns and inverted T-section cast iron beams supporting shallow brick arched floors. This revolutionary form of building (pioneered by Charles Bage) was obviously a success and, apart from the roof, the present building is still in its original 1805 condition. It even survived attacks during the war when the turbine area and dam received direct hits from 50 kg high explosive bombs. Work continued during the War as the Recruitment Poster (34) shows. Philip Zec (1910-83) designed the poster to recruit

women into factories up and down the country during the war. His artwork proved so successful that he is believed to have been on Hitler's hit list of people to be executed should Britain have been defeated.

In 1969 Armley Mills was purchased by Leeds City Council for conversion into an industrial museum for the region. In the collection is Matthew Murray's prototype for his Middleton Colliery locomotive (51) of 1812. Murray (35) was born at Stockton-on-Tees and came to Leeds in 1789 to work at Marshall's Scotland Mill. In 1795, with James Fenton and David Wood he founded the Round Factory at Holbeck where they produced textile machinery, steam engines and locomotives including the one illustrated. In 1804 he built Holbeck Lodge (locally known as Steam Hall) where he installed a steam central heating system a century and a half ahead of its time. During the Industrial Revolution many of the engineering pioneers were connected with Leeds. The 'father of civil engineering', John Smeaton, was educated at Leeds Grammar School and he is

represented on the panel with an engine (59) which had originally been designed by Thomas Newcomen in 1712. Smeaton then increased its efficiency by improving the sealing on the cylinders and individual parts measurements.

Armley Mills Museum also has a collection of printing presses including a cast-iron Columbian press (32) made by George Gaymer in 1845. This was donated to the museum by William Witts, the printers, when their premises were compulsorily purchased in 1973. William Witts was born in 1838, the year of the publication of 'Pickwick Papers'. His forefathers had been woollen cloth weavers but his father paid for the best education he could afford for his only son followed by an apprenticeship to the printing trade. The young William started his own business probably in 1871 and now his great grandson Roger Murgatroyd runs the company. One of the most daunting commissions the company has undertaken was to publish parts of the Bible, hymn books and spelling books in the African language of Ikongo. Three other printers are included here; Sunstreet (20) based in Keighley who offered their services, Small Print (45) a small firm in Chapel Allerton who have printed fliers and invitations for the Tapestry and Top Copy (33) who produced some of the first pieces printed on fabric.

Armley Mills played a part in the making of the Tapestry. When the project became too big for Kate's kitchen and studio and

34.
Recruitment Poster
Mary Sanders (5hrs)

59.
Smeaton's Engine
Anne Boyle

51.
Murray's Engine
Jan Brown (40hrs)

35.
Matthew Murray
Janet Carding(18hrs)

37.
James Hare's
Godfrey Harland (29hrs)

49.
Packaging
Betty Laycock (7hrs)

14.
James Hare Book
Elizabeth Thackrah
(2hrs)

had overflowed into the rest of the house, Daru Rooke, Director of the Museum, offered the Burling and Mending Room at the Mill. Many of the volunteers have fond memories of the time spent there with workshops and play days but it was time to move on when the lottery equipment arrived and more secure accomodation was needed.

Despite the decline of the textile industry in Leeds there are still many firms involved in the trade. One such company is Alfred Brown (Worsted Mills) Ltd (29) who came on board as sponsors. They were enthusiastic with ideas for their part of the panel and generous with their samples of fabric. The firm was founded in 1915 in Bramley, originally making uniforms for the police, fire brigades and the armed forces. Despite problems during the 1920s slump the firm survived, for many years producing cloth for Montague Burton. The business is now run by the fourth generation of the family. When the cloth halls were first built weaving was done by hand loom at home and now Alfred Brown's have 24 Sulzer looms which can produce 450 pieces per week (In the 1950s their 43 looms only produced 43 pieces per week). James Hare Silks (9,14), another family run firm, have been in business since the mid nineteenth century when the founder became a woollen and worsted merchant. In 1913 they began to make their

own cloth at Arlington Mill and built their warehouse in Queen Street (37). In 1973 'Hare of England' was sold to Illingworth Morris of Bradford, and the fourth generation of the family have continued in business as one of the largest distributors of silk in Europe. Their donated silks have been used on seven of the panels as the background and in many of the appliqued figures and buildings.

Peacock's, another firm established in the early nineteenth century had a shop on the corner of The Headrow and Park Row for over 100 years selling linos, carpets, curtains, loose covers, bedding and linen. They were at the retail end of the textile trade but did not have far to go to order goods as the packaging label illustrates (49). Founded in 1849 they moved in 1977 to their factory site at Kirkstall Bridge Mills and were taken over by Durastic Ltd in 1981. Mary Mawson worked in their sewing room for 26 years, approached the family to be sponsors and then went on to embroider the two pieces charted by Ann Wheatley (26,27). A panel representing Textiles of Leeds would not be complete without Marks and Spencer and Burtons. Michael Marks, a Polish Jewish immigrant came to Leeds to work for Barran. Instead he was loaned a small amount of money from which he established his Penny Bazaar in Leeds Market in 1884. Ten years later he went into partnership with Tom Spencer,

the cashier of a local mill. By 1905 they had opened seventy of their bazaars around the country. Montague Burton, also from Eastern Europe, started his clothing business in Chesterfield but in 1910 when he already had shops in many northern cities he moved to Leeds where he started manufacturing clothes as well as increasing his chain of shops. By the time of his death he was said to be clothing one-fifth of Britain's male population (13,17).

Other sponsors included show the variety of trades which played a part in the industrialisation of Leeds. Iron merchants John Stansfeld (36), were founded in 1859 selling goods manufactured from wood and steel. In Johnson's guide of 1889 they were referred to as one of the oldest established ironmongers in Yorkshire. Scattergood and Johnson (42), have supplied electrical goods for over a hundred years and now have branches in Gateshead, Manchester and Sheffield, as well as their head office in Lowfield Road. Johnson Radley (63) have been making moulds for producing glass bottles since 1919 and introduced us to their associated firm of Lax and Shaw who then make the end product. Between them they supplied perhaps the two most difficult images to embroider. Fortunately Betty Bertrand was equal to the challenge and like many other embroiderers involved found herself taking on work of the apparently impossible variety. Lax and

Shaw were established in 1891 primarily manufacturing pharmaceutical containers and later produced baby feeding bottles. When plastic baby bottles were introduced the firm changed direction and now supply colour coated glass ware such as the Sapphire Gin bottle (64). The firm also supplied some interesting historical documents, including a letter (62) from Lax & Shaw to the Army Recruiting Office, dated July 1916, asking for one of their men to be exempt from service, because he was too valuable to the firm. Clayton's are also a firm with long tradition. Their Managing Director chose this as his favourite image of one of their gas tanks erected in Morecambe. Their products are sold worldwide and its interesting to know that Kate's husband Brian started his world renowned Australian stamp collection because his grandfather, who worked as chief clerk for the firm in the 1930s, brought home the stamps from the company's envelopes.

In the nineteenth century Leeds was not only famed for its woollen cloth but was also the greatest leather producing town in Britain and one of these tanning factories belonged to Joseph Watson. The tallow extracted in the processing of the leather was sold as a by-product until Joseph's sons persuaded him to use it themselves to make soap. They were so successful that they soon had to build a new factory on Whitehall Road (43) and it was there, in the 1890s, that they introduced 'Matchless Cleanser' (46) a product which was advertised in a new and novel way. Everyone who sent in at least 30 wrappers from the product was guaranteed a prize and at its height the advertising campaign employed 250 people in the prize wrapper department, sending out 750,000 prizes a year. In 1917

27.
Peacock's Shop
Mary Mawson (106hrs)

42.
Scattergood & Johnson
Joan Holah

13.
Burton Montage
Betty Laycock (24hrs)

64.
Lax & Shaw
Betty Bertrand

50.
Garforth Colliery Barge
Joyce Maynard

43.
Elida Faberge
Kate Russell

56.
The Mallard
Eileen Wilson

46.
Elida Faberge
Betty Laycock (7hrs)

Joseph's grandson sold the firm to Levers and in 1930 it became part of the bigger Anglo-Dutch group Unilever. Soap production then began to be concentrated at Port Sunlight and toilet preparations at Joseph Watsons. Products such as Gibbs Fluoride, Pepsodent, Sunsilk and Clynol hairsprays and talcum powder from Pears have all been made at Whitehall Road works. Another successful advertising campaign within the group came from A & F Pears. They purchased the picture *Bubbles* (12) from Sir William Ingram who in turn had bought it from the artist Sir John Everett Millais to produce in the *Illustrated London News*. The portrait is of Sir John's grandson Willie James and at first he was angry that his work should be used in advertising. He was later pleased at the quality of the campaign. The Whitehall works closed in 1987 and the Leeds branch of the company moved to Seacroft. When the Textile panel was being planned the firm was called Elida Faberge and Evi Malm embroidered another soap boy (31) to include the parent company name.

All of the items of haberdashery, included on the panel both antique and modern, have come from the 'sewing boxes' of volunteers on the project. Each has its own story. The samples of weaving and their setts were donated by Margaret Clark and made by her father, John Heaps. He was born in 1894 and from starting at a mill at the age of 13 continued his education

including ATI at evening classes at Leeds University until in 1924 he became Designer at Edward Denison's in Yeadon. They manufactured cloth for ladies wear and supplied firms such as Marlbeck, Windsmoor, C&A and Gor-rey. He maintained that a fabric lacked quality if it left an impression of its weave on the thumb when pressed on it. Margaret took delight in buying clothes below his standard when she became independent, knowing they wouldn't wear forever! Margaret also donated the doyley (top left) with a wide band of tatting made by her Great Aunt, Eliza Firth, born in 1860. Asked how she could part with such an heirloom Margaret said that was easy, her Aunt's output was prolific, she didn't believe in idle hands and always had tatting and crochet on the go, stopping only on Sundays which were reserved for Chapel going or reading good books. Her mother was also an enthusiastic needlewoman but her embroideries are still in use so items from her work box have been used instead, including her spools of lisle thread for stocking repairs and her linen buttons.

The success of Leeds during and after the Industrial revolution relied on good transport links and this is covered on another panel with just a few representatives with Textiles and Industry. The Garforth Colliery Barge (50), Steam locomotive (54) and Electric trams (52,53) are all part of history now, though the Mallard (56) is still a crowd puller.

53.
Dougall's Tram
Margaret Clark (55hrs)

Not all of the pieces represent historical aspects of Leeds. Some of the sponsors are from relatively newly established firms. Clariant for instance is not a firm founded in Leeds but is a Swiss company who opened a chemical and pharmaceutical plant in Leeds in 1961, changing their name from Sandoz in 1997. Madeira Threads (UK) Limited were established in 1983 when the

MacPhersons began to sell this German make of embroidered thread. MKC were founded in 1958 and, as well as sewing machines, run the Bernina Club to support their customers. The newest machine they sell links directly to the internet to download patterns, has a repertoire of 800 stitches and has an automatic thread cutter!

The embroiderers among us will be familiar with Bonds of Farsley. The shop front (21) illustrated looks normal enough, but step inside (22) and it resembles an Aladdins cave, spreading over four rooms. Mr & Mrs Bond generously opened an account for the volunteers who could go to get materials for working on the Tapestry without paying. Part of the project's bartering system for their shop to be represented on the panel and, we suspect, more than generous. It may have been emphasised that it was

hard to get sponsors, but it should also be stated that some exceeded all expectations. When Drusilla White from Duttons for Buttons (15) heard about the project she asked Kate to contact her when the Textile panel was underway so that the shops could be represented.

One of the most enthusiastic firms was Hopkins Catering Equipment. They were contacted via Bryan's Fish Restaurant. As well as the family running the business the whole family got involved with the Tapestry, providing a cartoon to bring to life the story of the Fish Fryer. Neither did Mrs Hopkins forget us when a neighbouring tailor retired and she rescued his cloth for tapestry use.

Other sponsors also became involved in the whole project rather than the one piece. Mr Sumner of the Clothworker's Guild provided a host of beautiful images to be used on the Education Panel and also gave us the picture of the teasel to enhance the *Pins & Needles* panel and information on how to contact all of the other guilds. This resulted in The Painters and Stainers (7) and the Draper's Company (8) coming on board. These livery companies were founded before the Industrial Revolution (the first reference to the Painters and Stainers was as early as 1283) but are still relevant today supporting charities and promoting education.

Perhaps this panel more than any other reflects the culture and the formative years of the City – or maybe we love it just because we are textile fans!

15.
Duttons for Buttons
Vicky Storr

Teasels

A Picture of Health

1. Leeds University
Janet Taylor (12hrs)

2. Environmental Health
Beverley Silverman

3. Leeds Hospital Fund
Renee Silverman (5hrs)

4. Macmillan Cancer Relief
Eileen Wilson

5. St James & Seacroft
Barbara Walker (5hrs)

6. Nuffield Hospitals
Barbara Walker (3hrs)

7. B & N Housing
Ena Dunn

8. Hospital Fund
Renee Silverman

9. Leeds Hospital Fund
Elizabeth Thackrah (2hrs)

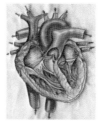
10. Brain
Ena Dunn (5.5hrs)

11. Leeds Health
Barbara Walker (3hrs)

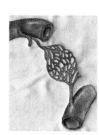
12. Heart
Anne Cove

13. School of Medicine
Linda Smith

14. Arteries & Veins
Sally Walton

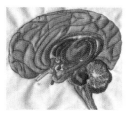
15. DNA
Barbara Walker (5hrs)

16. Nuffield Institute
Ena Dunn (4hrs)

17. Eye
Anne Cove (5.5hrs)

18. Heart Research
Barbara Walker (2hrs)

19. Ear
Anne Cove (5.5hrs)

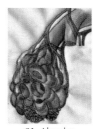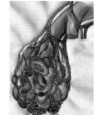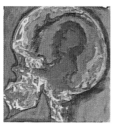
20. Hand
Anne Cove (3.6hrs)

21. Alveolus
Barbara & Jessica Walker

22. Kirlian Skull
Elizabeth Thackrah

23. Bandaging Arm
Janet Taylor (12hrs)

24. Pulses
Elizabeth Thackrah (4hrs)

Page 46

25. Nurses League
Barbara Walker

26. Surgeries Map
Sally Walton

27. Leeds Teaching Hospitals
Eileen Cummings

28. University of Leeds
Janet Taylor

29. Kidney Patients
Sally Walton

30. The Caducaeus
Renee Silverman (5hrs)

31. Pharmacy Cross
Myra Turner (2.5hrs)

32. Phrenology
Elizabeth Thackrah (5.5hrs)

33. Gene Diagram
Linda Smith

34. Radiography
Myra Turner ((4.5hrs)

35. Distillery
Ena Dunn (12hrs)

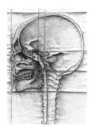

36. Leonardo's Skull
Anne Cove (6hrs)

37. Urn & Serpent
Sally Walton

38. Hippocrate
Linda Smith (6hrs)

39. Baby Scan
Sally Holmes

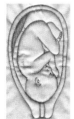

39. Baby in Womb
Linda Smith

40. Staff & Serpent
Linda Smith (5hrs)

41. Esculape
Barbara Walker (3hrs)

42. Pestle & Mortar
Barbara Walker (3hrs)

43. Bandaged Hand
Anne Cove

44. Hands Sample
Beverley Silverman

45. Sample
Anne Cove

46. Leeds Dental School
Elizabeth Thackrah (5hrs)

47. Sample
Anne Cove

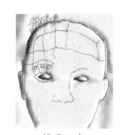

48. Sample
Beverley Silverman

49. Sample
Carol Wilson

50. Sample
Anne Cove

51. Sample
Anne Cove

52. Sample
Anne Cove

IN OBJECTS PRESENTED

53. Lettering by the team
54. Nuffield Hospitals
Barbara Walker

Angel Detail
Anne Cove

43.
Bandaged Hand
Anne Cove

3.
Leeds Hospital Fund
Renee Silverman (5hrs)

This panel had almost as tortuous a route to completion as did *Faith in Leeds*. Much of the research, discussion and fund-raising had been completed by 1998 but other elements of the project were by this time so overwhelming that the possibility of 'space of mind' for designing seemed out of the question.

Frances Ledgard, former Press Officer at Leeds University, early in the process had gathered together the schools and departments of the University devoted to aspects of health care. Due to her rallying work many fruitful meetings and discussions had been held, both at Armley Mills and in the departments themselves. Several folders full of annual reports, brochures, medical pamphlets and illustrations, plus Kate's own photographs of hospital buildings, had been collected. It was extremely frustrating for her not to be able to get on with the design since, as always, there were volunteers ready and willing to do the embroidery and sponsors eager to see the work they had paid for.

The first sponsor to come on board was the Leeds Hospital Fund through the company secretary, Angela Romaine. Being a needle woman herself she saw the potential for the Fund's involvement, and later in the life of this panel when it was in need of a transfusion, she arranged for a further injection of funds.

In 1998 Kate approached the Board of Trustees with the idea that another artist be commissioned to design the panel to represent health. She had in mind Paddy Killer whose work she knew and had long admired and who has many connections with the region. It was very exciting when both the Board of Trustees and Paddy herself agreed to the proposal that she be commissioned not only to design the panel, but to run a series of master classes. In these classes she would teach already experienced artists and machinists to work in her impeccable style. The first weekend workshop was chaotic, so many people had signed up that Paddy found it difficult to make herself heard against the general din. Embroiderers learning new techniques can sometimes behave like small children on Christmas morning. Paddy was probably relieved to find that over the months the number of volunteers dwindled to a more manageable size.

The awarding of the Arts Council Lottery grant to buy state of the art computerised sewing machines and Applemac computers coincided with Paddy joining the technological age with her Apple G3. She had great ideas of using the

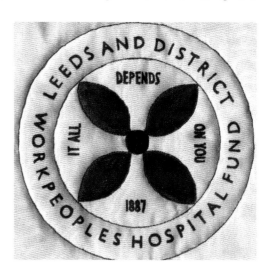

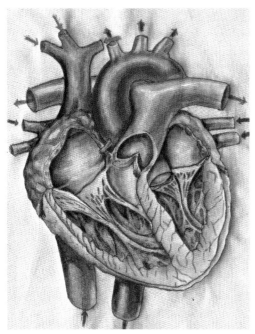

computer to alter and print the images but was used to working with a stable machine on her desk at home. The volunteers, on the other hand, had to keep the computers in boxes in a cupboard at Armley Mills and set them up without technicians (none available at the weekend), never having dealt with Applemacs before. One particular weekend was so frustrating that, after Beverley Silverman's husband was called out to assist but was unable to sort the problem, Barbara Walker kidnapped one of the machines to see if she could make sense of it at home. This of course was the grand idea! That volunteers would be able to loan, on a short or long term basis, equipment with which to pursue personal research or development. This would also, of course, benefit the project in terms of production and experimentation and in terms of sharing the knowledge gained with other volunteers. In this case it turned into a long-term loan, leading on to the manipulation and collaging of photographs on many of the other panels and the compilation of the database.

Over the first few 'master classes' the small team of volunteers, who would later become 'the management team', identified themselves and took notes and worked samples to Paddy's exacting standards. Everyone was impressed with the generosity with which she shared the tips, techniques and secrets of her profession and with the rigour with which she insisted that samples be done again, and again (see 45, 47, 50, 51 - each at least 18 inches tall).

The technology and the design gradually came together and in 1999 the result was shown to the various health professionals, bodies and organisations for final discussion and approval. Although the search for sponsors was still going on and many institutions it had been intended to portray on the panel had declined the opportunity sufficiently often for the message to sink in, it was becoming urgent that a conclusion

12.
Heart
Anne Cove

15.
DNA
Barbara Walker (5hrs)

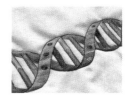

50.
Sample
Anne Cove

39.
Baby Scan
Sally Holmes

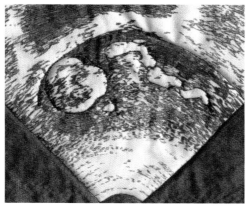

21.
Alveolus
Barbara & Jessica
Walker

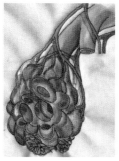

Anne Cove putting
finishes touches to the
panel.

was reached in order to begin the work. The nature of the construction of this panel meant that the design had to be complete before production could even begin.

Then - Shock! Horror! - some of the professionals did not like the design. Their objections were fundamental, they did not like the classical approach and felt that the panel should have a more modern appearance. Some felt strongly enough to withdraw participation and funds unless changes were made. This was a very serious blow - for Paddy, for all the volunteers working on the panel and for Kate. Paddy had already worked more than the time she was paid for and also had other commitments. The small core of volunteers who remained were still interested in being involved but were unsure of how to proceed with the change of design and so Kate's hoped for arms-length involvement was dashed; she was firmly at the helm again. One of the criticisms of the first design was that we did not use sufficient images of new technology. Such images had been requested from all organisations early in the process but the ones produced had little or no visual or design merit. Paddy and her team had attempted to fill this gap, spending hours on various web sites and visiting libraries with little success. One of the most difficult tasks for an artist is to take over from another, altering parts yet still

keeping the design qualities of the first. The panel became a bit of an albatross over the next few months, always there to be tackled with Kate looking for solutions to the problem and the volunteers not knowing which bits were being kept which they could get on with.

In order that *A Picture of Health* would not stand out as something completely different from the other panels, Kate had sketched *Education* as its companion. It was when this panel's design had been completed that she finally found a visual connection with *A Picture of Health* and a sense of having something to contribute. Eventually through Gail Bolland, Director of Tonic and her colleague Tim Vernon, plus Frances Ledgard, and Brian Wilson of South Leeds Art College who loaned medical books from his college library, sufficient imagery was found to restructure the lower half of the panel. Fortunately Kate was able to commission Paddy to draw up the foreground figures to maintain continuity with the rest of the design.

Six of the group who had attended the original master classes were still, three years on, able and willing to attempt the often daunting task of producing the revised design. Elizabeth Thackrah and Kate managed to pressgang another four, including Sally Holmes who brought with her a scan of her pre-birth daughter (39) which was embroidered for the border.

Paddy Killer works with precision. She produces hundreds of samples before embarking on a new project and knows exactly how much shrinkage occurs with each fabric she uses depending on the density of stitches. It had been intended that she would stitch together all the sections made by the volunteers. In her absence it was decided to have as few pieces in the main panel as possible to make joining the pieces relatively uncomplicated but this meant that the bulk of the work was done by two people. Anne Cove painted the top and bottom sections, including nursing and medical staff photographed by Kate, with detail of the uniforms from the archive of St James's Hospital. She also painted her daughter-in-law, Jo, representing Flora a symbol of blooming health. Tim Vernon, who supplied the images also allowed us to use one of his original pieces of artwork (20)

Three years on from kidnapping the Applemac, Barbara had now become capable of altering photographs. She produced the images of the helicopter and dental school to add to the hospital buildings first drawn by Paddy and skilfully transferred to silk, painted and quilted by Sally Walton. The buildings are from the left: Leeds General Infirmary with the Dental School behind and on the right St James Hospital in front of the Brotherton wing of

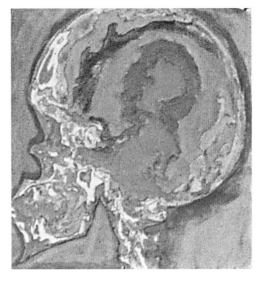

22.
Kirlian Skull
Elizabeth Thackrah

the LGI. When the three sections had been completed it took a whole day to tack them together, then Elizabeth united them by doing miles of vermicelli for the background and finally Janet Taylor joined all the pieces together.

After all this time it appeared the troubles were over but there were more to come. The finished piece was too wide to fit on the frame. Despite working to precise measurements to include shrinkage from quilting, there were too many variables caused by so many different people doing the work but the volunteers learned to appreciate the precision needed in Paddy's own work.

The core group of 'stitchers down' were brilliant at this stage. They brought fresh enthusiasm to getting the piece onto the frame including creating a new twill backing, an extra layer of wadding and losing particularly loose bits with a technique not unlike 'Suffolk puffs'. Eventually the piece more or less reached the desired finished proportions. Having struggled so much it is even more gratifying when an observer, blissfully ignorant of all the trials, showers praise on the whole team and declares this panel to be his or her favourite.

23.
Bandaging arm
Janet Taylor

30.
The Caducaeus
Renee Silverman (5hrs)

1. Leeds Grammar School Elevation by Barbara Walker (25hrs)

2. Parkinson Building, University of Leeds, by Janet Taylor (24hrs)

3. Clothworkers' Court, University of Leeds
Myra Turner

4. Leeds Metropolitan University
Denise Teed

5. Swarthmore
Janet Taylor (6hrs)

6. Yorkshire Ladies Council
Ruth Lawrence & E. Cummings

7. Students
Janet Taylor (1.5hrs)

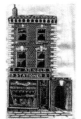

8. E.J. Arnold's
Joan Holah (20hrs)

9. Hollingworth & Moss
Pauline Clayden (24.5hrs)

10. Samples
Chris Richardson

11. Clouds
Chris Richardsom

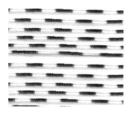

12. Edge Stitching
B Bertrand & E Thackrah

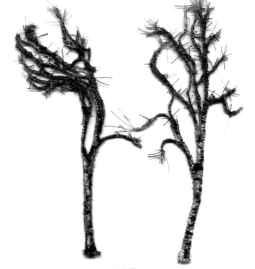

16. Trees
Denise Teed

13. Quilting sample
Chris Richardson

NINE TENTHS OF EDUCATION IS ENCOURAGEMENT

14. Lettering
Elizabeth Thackrah (31hrs)

15. White board
Janet Taylor

17. Small People by Denise Teed

18. Moorlands Pupils
Sheila Exley

19. Victoria & Erica Ballantyne
Betty Bertrand

20. Claire Thirlwell
Mrs D Thirlwell

21. Anne Louse Hargreaves
Susan Hargreaves

22. Leeds Girl's High School

23. Moorlands Pupil
Sheila Exley

24. Philippa Randall

25. Mrs Karen Taylor
Karen Taylor

26. Mr C Brian Best
Angela Mason

27. Toni Bolton
Janet Taylor

28. Jean Hertzog
Janet Taylor

29. Bernadette Wade
Janet Taylor

30. Menike Kumarasena
Janet Taylor

31. Dr Owen
Rosemary Hargreaves

32. Sarah Berry
Betty Bertrand

33. O.U. Graduate
Janet Taylor

34. Daniel, Megan and Gareth Chambers
Margaret Chambers

35. Garforth Community College
Zuber Mohammed and team

36. Open University
Beryl Smith

37. College of Art & Design
Jan Webster (56hrs)

38. The Clothworkers'' Company
Jane Dew

39. Intake High School
Joyce James

40. Leeds Training Trust
Janet Carding

41. Leeds Civic Trust
Minnie Woodward (62hrs)

42. Leeds Heritage Trail
Lesley Dove (40hrs)

43. Westfield Junior School
Joyce James

44. Moorlands School
Margaret Milne (100hrs)

45. Miles Hill Primary
Lesley Dove

46. Park Spring Primary
Pauline Clayden

47. Hollingworth & Moss
Gill Cook

48. The University of Leeds
Gill Cook

49. Trinity & All Saints
Barbara Hebden (8hrs)

50. LMU
Dorothy Wrench (16hrs)

51. LMU
Joyce James

52. LCC Crest
Barbara Gray

53. LMU
Val Gomersall

54. LMU
Valerie Horner (43hrs)

55. Leeds Grammar School
Mary Mellor

56. Gateways School
Sheila Smith

57. Gledhow Primary
Dorothy Wrench

58. Fulneck School
Margaret Milne (56hrs)

59. Rawdon Littlemoor
Pauline Dean (7hrs)

60. Leeds Girls' High
Janet Carding

61. Intake School
Joan Moore (55hrs)

62. St Mary's School
Roberta Bamforth

63. Yorkshire College
Barbara Gray (30hrs)

64. Fuller's Teasel
Elizabeth Thackrah (6hrs)

65. Association of Secretaries
Margery Hill

66. Open University
Eileen Cummings

67. South Leeds Art College
Joan Holah (8hrs)

68. Leeds Express
Brenda Archer

69. Women's Institute

70. Gildersome Primary
Val Gomersall

71. Association of Women Graduates
Joyce James

72. Park Lane
Cynthia Shipley

73. Open College Network
Joyce James

74. Leeds College of Music

75. Janet Taylor
Janet Taylor (8hrs)

76. I Too Project
Judith Reynolds & J Taylor

77. Headingley Primary
School Badge

78. Books
Dorothy Wrench (2hrs)

79. Girl with Easel
Helen Parrott (15hrs)

80. Carolyn Wild
Betty Bertrand (7hrs)

81. Jane Stephenson
Betty Bertrand (10hrs)

82. Recorder Group
Jackie Ford

83. Boy at Blackboard
Margaret Clark

84. Richard Hoggart
Nell Adams (16hrs)

85. Robin & Lesley Dove
Lesley Dove

86. Mr A. Daville
Angela Mason

87. Park Spring Pupil
Margaret Clark

88. Singer (SLAC)
Jan Webster (10hrs)

89. LGHS pupil
Pamela Kirby

90. Sophie & James
Pauline Clayden (8hrs)

91. Miles Hill Pupils
Muriel Gabbitas (15hrs)

92. Girl Clapping
Sheila Exley

93. Kate Williams
Val Gomersall (8hrs)

94. Keith Brotherton Moore
Godfrey Harland

95. Keely
Rosie Kearton (20hrs)

96. Rosie Kearton
Janet Taylor (6hrs)

97. Merel Jackson
Merel Jackson (8.5hrs)

98. Marina Edwards
Janet Taylor

99. Kelly Trotter
Sheila Exley

100. Alan Rosentjorn
Janet Taylor

101. Brian Peace
Janet Taylor

102. Kate Russell
Janet Taylor

103. Victoria Russell
Janet Taylor (5hrs)

104. Maria Spellacy
Audrey Gabbitas (50hrs)

105. West Side Story players
Ann Boyle (50hrs)

106. Mr G O' Donnell
Jackie Ford

107. Joanna
Joan Holah (12hrs)

108. Clare Short MP
Val Gomersall (37hrs)

109. Sue Kershaw
Janet Taylor (4hrs)

110. L. Brayshaw
Janet Taylor (5hrs)

111. Girl with brick
Janet Taylor (6hrs)

112. Mark Best
Janet Taylor (7hrs)

113. Rawdon Littlemoor Pupil
Rosalind Kirk

114. Performing Arts
Janet Taylor (12hrs)

115. Park Spring Pupil
Margaret Haynes & J Taylor

117. Girl with Tiara
Anne Cove

116. David Thornton
Ann Boyle

121. Two Sisters

118. Jane & Sylvia Crowther
Janet Taylor (5.5hrs)

119. Gateways Pupil
Janet Taylor

120. Girl with Hat
Janet Taylor

Education

Research and fund-raising began in 1994 whilst one of the Tapestry workspaces was still in a vacant shop unit in the Victoria Quarter. Frances Ledgard, then Press Officer at Leeds University, visited Kate many times with other of her colleagues, expressing an interest in sponsoring both the *Education* and *Picture of Health* panels.

It was always Kate's intention to have these panels displayed next to each other and have some visual links in the designs. It seemed obvious to her that *education* had to be as much about people as institutions and show learning in its broadest sense. However, it was still necessary to find sufficient sponsorship and represent the major institutions of Education. From Kate's 25 years working in education and her discussions with potential sponsors, an image emerged. Schools and colleges occupied the top section of the panel with graduates of all forms of learning bursting, thronging and bustling to the foreground, many holding or wearing items to suggest the various forms of education available.

There were hundreds of such dialogues and 1,000 letters were sent out, with a sketch plan of the panel, to Leeds schools, colleges etc. Only five institutions expressed an interest. As with the other panels, the positive responses were from people already involved in the project or the people they in turn had contacted.

During 1997/8, frustrated at the lack of progress and having a sponsor and two volunteers eager to get started, Kate took a risk. She started producing a design for the Grammar School based on her preliminary idea that buildings would be depicted from which crowds would spill forth; something in the style of the *Community Spirit* Panel. When Paddy Killer who was producing the design for the *Picture of Health* panel revealed her concept, Kate realised she would need to revise her idea and create a more formal structure to reflect the design of the *Picture of Health* panel. The two volunteers, Ann Barker and Mary Mellor, were very understandably upset and annoyed that their piece would not be used in this panel and an attempt to include it in the *Community Spirit* panel was foiled by lack of space. During the course of the project some other pieces have also not been used including leaves and people. These were overproduced at workshops or some pieces were made twice, all beautifully embroidered but

34.
Daniel, Megan and Gareth Chambers
Margaret Chambers

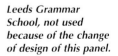

Leeds Grammar School, not used because of the change of design of this panel.

without a home. None of them will be wasted. The *Serendipity* panel will be made in the future when volunteers will be invited to share their design skills

The revised design format was ready in early 1999. Details were still to be added as the search was continuing for sponsors, coats of arms and school badges for the border sections. Also needed were actual people to swell the crowds issuing from the University of Leeds Parkinson building.

Many of the photographs received at the Tapestry office could not be used. Some were too small, others unfocussed or lacking 'life'. Assisted by various volunteers including Councillor Graham Latty (then a Trustee of the Tapestry) some beautifully clear prints were received from Rawdon Littlemoor Primary School (113). Melissa Wilde and Rachel Myers (76) of the *I Too* project also contributed good photographs and Cllr Latty came up with a school photograph of his grandchildren (91). Park Spring Primary School (27, 87, 110, 111, 112, 115 and 116) where one of the volunteers used to teach, also produced a brilliant set of images of children's activities.

When nearing the deadline for completion

and still several people short of a crowd Kate began asking everyone she knew and met if they had been educated in Leeds and if she could photograph them for the panel. Sarah Berry (32) a student from Kate's *tai chi* class and a philosophy graduate provided a great set of 'action' shots of her striding optimistically into the future. Several photos were taken by Kate on her many research treks around Chapel Allerton and its cemetery. For example Mr O'Donnell (106) educated at Chapel Allerton, St Anne's and St Augustine's and Mr Davile (87) educated at Sheepscar School. An image of Kate leaping out from behind gravestones springs to mind here but she assures us that she behaved with perfect decorum!

People associated with the Tapestry were also included. Merel Jackson (98), a member of the volunteer 'core' group and a student at Mary Lord's famous painting class at Swarthmore, carries one of the artist's paintings which will appear on the *Arts for All* panel. Victoria Russell (104), Kate's daughter, just had to be included. Educated

76.
I Too Project
Judith Reynolds
& J Taylor

113.
***Rawdon Littlemoor
Pupil***
Rosalind Kirk

2.
***Parkinson Building,
University of Leeds***
Janet Taylor (24hrs)

32. Top Right
Sarah Berry
Betty Bertrand

at Aireborough Grammar School and St Martin's College she won the prestigious BP Portrait Award of the Year while the panel was being made. She then went on to paint the tree shadows on the *Faith in the City* panel! Fundraiser Sylvia Crowther (118) appears at her daughter's graduation as does Rosie Kearton (95, 96) who was employed as Project Manager for a time when the Tapestry was at Holy Trinity Church. Janet Taylor (75) appears at her own graduation and Robin and Lesley Dove (86) are there taking notes which is appropriate to Robin's role as one of the researchers for the project. Kate's husband Brian (101) is a governor of the Northern School of Contemporary Dance and representing the school are Marina Edwards, Kelly Trotter and Alan Rosentjorn (98-100).

Philippa Randall (24), former headmistress of Leeds Girls High School, who appears with a school governor (26), parent (25) and pupils, was extraordinarily helpful in working with Kate to create interest throughout the school community. This resulted in several workshops being held at the school and at Armley Mills Museum in which parents and pupils were encouraged to create a stitched portrait of themselves or their family (20, 21, 22, 25). The portraits of some of the pupils and Sue Braithwaite, then a teacher at Leeds Girls High School, together with her family appear on the *Civic Pride* panel as a result of these workshops. These links between panels are legion and sometimes made keeping the database hazardous!

Bernadette Wade, who appears with three colleagues (28, 29, 30, 33) representing the Open University, thought she would be able to interest the OU administration in funding

the representation of the Academic Crest. She was surprised to meet resistance but undaunted, proceeded to enlist the support of other graduates in having the OU appear on the panel (36). It is entirely due to her persistence that this happened.

Many design ideas came from overcoming problems. Kate recalls David Hockney, a contemporary of hers at Bradford College of Art, saying that a palm appeared in one of his paintings because he had trouble drawing hands (or was it feet!).

Sections of the *Education* panel are monochromatic and pieced to make a link with Paddy's cream and dark grey silk quilt. The sections that are full colour and applique are to link with other panels. Many crests supplied by sponsors were in only black and white, so the border was created with the lower half monochrome and the upper half in colour to balance the centre panel where this pattern was reversed. Buildings were embroidered in black and white to indicate that they are simply the shell, the 'housing', of education. The people, in full glorious colour and in three dimensions, are the product and life of the education process.

117.
Girl with Tiara
Anne Cove

25.
Mrs Karen Taylor
Karen Taylor

123.
Trinity and All Saints
Pauline Dean (6hrs)

38.
The Clothworkers'
Company
Jane Dew

64.
Fuller's Teasel
Elizabeth Thackrah
(6hrs)

3.
Clothworkers' Court,
Leeds University
Myra Turner

The resulting design of the *Education* panel created technical problems. Kate's quilting experience and skills were not equal to directing others in collating the process. She therefore had to rely on expertise from volunteers to put together the thirty sections of embroidered shields and badges and the centre panel. By December 2001, seriously behind the deadline, Kate turned in desperation to Chris Richardson of the *Night Owls* quilters. On Christmas Day she delivered the many sections to Chris, who amazingly dropped her other commitments (including her husband's Christmas present) and worked over the festive season, adjusting, extending and willing the wayward pieces into one.

There were other technical problems. How could the many quotations selected be fitted into the exact shape and size of the two border sections? Chris Ratcliffe of Pennine Pens Web Design literally filled the gap for us here and on the *Picture of Health* panel. It was a great shame that in the final stitching of Education, there was just no room for the outer border. The decorative dotted-line borders were another problem; solved in this case by machine-stitching space-dyed thread onto pelmet vilene and tearing off the thereby perforated 'strips' to applique separately onto the panel by hand after the text border (12).

Mr Sumner from the Clothworkers' Foundation was exceptionally generous with his time in finding good images for pieces on the panel. He supplied so much information and history about the company that this book could be filled with it alone. Briefly, the Clothworkers' Company was incorporated by Royal Charter in 1528 as an amalgamation of The Fullers' and The Shearmen's Companies. The Company was granted the Coat of Arms in 1530 and the crest and supporters in 1587. The arms represent the hissicks and teasels used in cloth working. The golden ram represents the wealth and success obtainable from wool and the supporters are griffins. Jane Dew is a professional embroiderer who specialises in goldwork and after she had run several enjoyable workshops everyone was delighted that she worked this piece (38). The Clothworkers' Court (3) is also featured on the panel. In 1874 the Company helped to found the Yorkshire College of Science by making a grant to build the Department of Textile Industries. They added to this six years later with the Department of 'Tinctorial Chemistry', now known as Colour Chemistry and Dyeing. The Teasel in the border of the panel was also taken from a bas-relief on the building. Historically teasels have been used to bring up a lustrous polished nap or pile on certain cloths before the final finishing process. Despite centuries of improvement in production of cloth nothing has been invented to take the place of this plant.

The Yorkshire College of Science became an independent University in 1904 (for several years it had been part of the Victoria University in Manchester). In 1937 Frank Parkinson, 'an old boy', donated £200,000 to build an imposing entrance to the campus and that building is named after him (2). The city's other University was formed by many institutions amalgamating and is represented on the panel not only by the Brunswick building (4) from the 1960s but also by several now historic logos. Immediately prior to the founding of the Polytechnic the Leeds City Council crest (52) was used by various of the colleges. Carnegie College (54) had its own crest before amalgamation in 1976 as did Yorkshire College of Education and Home Economics (63) and City of Leeds College (50).

The panel celebrates life long learning and one of the most respected institutes upholding this principle is Swarthmore (5). Established in 1909 and in Woodhouse Square since 1919, the centre was started by a Quaker family who named it after Swarthmore Hall in Cumbria. They run evening and day classes on almost anything for which there is a demand.

School days are represented by the architect's elevation of the new Grammar School Building. The Institution itself is first recorded in 1552 though it may have been founded as early as 1341. This building however was first opened to pupils in September 1997. Embroidering the piece was not easy. Attempts at hand and machine stitching had to be aborted, the long straight lines were impossible to keep straight on such an open weave fabric and machine thread was too thin to be seen properly. Eventually it was all done in

83.
Boy at Blackboard
Margaret Clark

4. above left
Leeds Metropolitan University
Denise Teed

couching using perle thread. The school's badge is also on the panel. Adopted around 1820 the motto is *The Mother of All Knowledge* and the three books are said to be Homer, Virgil/Euclid and the New Testament.

Books and paper, essentials for education, were supplied for over a hundred years by E J Arnold. Founded in 1863 in Barnstaple, the company moved to Briggate (8) in 1870 as printers, stationers, publishers and suppliers of materials to local schools. The trade expanded rapidly with the passing of the 1902 Education Act giving free education to all children. By the 1980's the fourth generation were running the business with over 1,000 staff and with a market extending throughout England and abroad, particularly Africa. The images of the recorder group (83) and the boy at the blackboard (84) are from one of E J Arnold's old catalogues. Olav Arnold not only supplied the images but popped in from time to time to see how work was progressing and finally gave much help and support in producing the two books.

One of the final images of buildings used is that of the Yorkshire Ladies Council of Education, in Blenheim Terrace. Yorkshire Ladies was founded in 1876 to promote the education of girls and women. The other is that of Hollingworth and Moss, Academic Bookbinders.

50.
LMU
Dorothy Wrench
(16hrs)

58.
Fulneck School
Margaret Milne (56hrs)

1. Girl Skipping
Val Gomersall

2. Carnival Queen
Godfrey Harland (17hrs)

3. Lady in Sharara
Jean Webber

4. Bharata Natyam Dance
Margaret Clark (39.5hrs)

5. Orissi Dance
Thelma Manning (30hrs)

6. Bharata Natyam Dance
Victoria Russell (35hrs)

7. 'Little Star'
Susan Timblin

8. Carnival Boy
Godfrey Harland (68hrs)

9. 'Little Bee'
Eileen Cummings (4.5hrs)

10. Morris Dancers
Betty Bertrand (30hrs)

11. Morris Dancers
Val Gomersall (28hrs)

12. Yorkshire Dance
Ena Dunn (7hrs)

13. Traveller's Children
Sue Evans (40hrs)

14. Girls with Crowns
Merel Jackson (15hrs)

15. Playhouse Dressing-up
Jackie Moore (28hrs)

16. Two Clowns
Janet Taylor

17. The Mikado
Margaret Clark (19.5hrs)

18. Katisha
Margaret Milne (20hrs)

19. 'Have a Nice Day'
Godfrey Harland (18hrs)'

20. Chinese Dragon
Renee Silverman (200hrs)

21. Chinese Children
Mary Mawson (56hrs)

22. See-saw at Martin House
Valerie Horner (11hrs)

23. Boy from Lincoln Green
Barbara Hebden (5hrs)

24. Girl from Lincoln Green
Barbara Hebden (5.5hrs)

25. Soroptomists Banner
Merel Jackson (40hrs)

26. Yorkshire Water by
Joyce Maynard
27. Foyle & Kirk by Joyce
James

28. Bus Stop
Joyce Maynard

29. Happy Vaisakhi by
Merel Jackson (26hrs)
30. Helping Hands by
Barbara Farrugia (3hrs)

31. Association of Secretaries
Margery Hill (20hrs)

32. Intake High School
Laura Hebden (2hrs)

33. Martin House
Judith Reynolds (12hrs)

34. Leeds G & S Society
Pauline Clayden

35. Aireborough G & S Society
Joyce James

36. Rambling Club
Eileen Gibb (4hrs)

37. Girl's Brigade
Beverley Harvey (10hrs)

38. Boys' Brigade
Brenda Archer (5hrs)

39. Latch
Jackie Moore (4hrs)

40. Leeds Voice
Brenda Archer

41. New Working Ways
Joan Holah (15hrs)

42. Yorkshire Water by
Maureen Elvidge
43. Chinese Text Banner
Joan Holah (10hrs)

44. Association of Wrens
Commercial Badge

45. Evans of Leeds
Brenda Archer (6hrs)

46. HSBC Logo
Joyce Maynard

47. Nurses League
June Adams

48. Chinese Women's Group
Julia Cooper (1.5hrs)

49. B & N Housing
Jackie Moore (4hrs)

50. Principles Logo by
Jenny McLean (1hr)
51. Evans Logo by Esta
Andrews (2.5hrs)

52. Common Purpose
Barbara Walker (1hr)

53. Clifford Brooke Centre
Ena Dunn (3.5hrs)

54/55 NSPCC
Children by Julia Cooper
(2hrs)

56. Roscoe Luncheon Club
Joyce James

57. H.A.O.S.
Eileen Gibb (25hrs)

58. Latin American Banner
Gloria Rhodes (10hrs)

59. Boy with Diabalo
Gwen Woolliscroft (5hrs)

60. Jane Hustwit
Janet Taylor (3.5hrs)

61. Rob Bumby
Janet Taylor (3.5hrs)

62. Clown
Margaret Clark (29hrs)

63. Boy with Ball
Gwen Woolliscroft (8hrs)

64. Man with Accordion
Sandra Sutton

65. Lady Singing
Sally Lindley (24.5hrs)

66. Holy Trinity Cafe Staff
Janet Taylor

67. Holy Trinity Cafe Staff
Joan Moore (23hrs)

68. Audrey Pidgeon
Joan Holah (14hrs)

69. Chess Player
Denise Teed (5hrs)

70. Irish Dancer
Jan Brown

71. Boy from Lincoln Green
Hilary Thurlow (14hrs)

72. Staff from Armley Mills
Claire Wildman

73. Town Crier
Valerie Horner (16hrs)

74. Ian Adams
Karen Pattison (6hrs)

75. Miss Mackintosh (1)
Beryl Mayhew

76. Miss Mackintosh (2)
Rosie Kearton (8hrs)

77. Danny Freeman
Sheila Exley

78. Tap Dancer
Val Gomersall

79. Boy with Violin
Pat Potton (40hrs)

Chinese Musicians
Betty Bertrand (8hrs)

81. Two Singers
Joan Holah (40hrs)

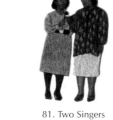
82. Two more Singers
Joan Holah (40hrs)

83. Louise Read
Sheila Exley

84. Library Chess Set
Denise Teed (15hrs)

85. LS 2000 Logo
Angela Turner

86. Maypole
Pauline Clayden (15.5hrs)

87. Sky & Fireworks
Jack Marlowe (239hrs)

88. Singapore Dragon
Eileen Wilson

89. Boys' Brigade
Merel Jackson (10.5hrs)

90. Greek Dancers
Anne Boyle (45hrs)

91. Musicians at Mela
June Hardy (7hrs)

92. Kate & Betty
Betty Bertrand

93. Morris Men
Merel Jackson (6.5hrs)

94. Cameraman & Boy
Jackie Ford (8hrs)

95. Arthur France & Friends
Sheila Exley & Jean Nichols

96. 'Youth at Risk' Team
Myra Turner (13hrs)

97. Ana Sylvia Rodriguez
Liz Firth & Victoria Russell

98. Latin Americans
Liz Firth (10hrs)

99. Hoop & Ball Players
Judith Baron

100. Matron Jean Walker
Val Gomersall

101. Musicians at Swarthmore
Janet Taylor (4.5hrs)

102. 'Black Elders' Ladies
Janet Taylor (12hrs)

103. Messrs Rakusen
Joan Holah (20hrs)

104. Youth at Risk
Hilary Thurlow (18hrs)

105. Two Lady Travellers
Barbara Hebden (14.5hrs)

106. Carol with Owl
Mary Smith (6hrs)

107. 2000 Father & Daughter
Gloria Rhodes (20hrs)

108. Ada North
Ann Brown (24hrs)

109. Veronica & her Dad
Veronica Dore

110. Lady in flowery blouse
Joyce James

111. Mr Baron & Grandchild
Mrs Baron

112. Gospel Singer
Victoria Russell (30hrs)

113. Ayesha Dost
Arshima & Ayesha Dost

114. Three Sikh Men
Godfrey Harland (32hrs)

115. Girls at Lincoln Green
Hilary Thurlow (18hrs)

116. TSB Balloons
Joyce James (6hrs)

117. Red Injuns
Jackie Ford (20hrs)

118. Carnival Queen
M. Clark & Audrey Pidgeon

119. Girl in Pink
Janet Taylor (6hrs)

120. Girl in Red
June Hardy (5hrs)

121. 'Tiger' Boy
Renee Silverman (12hrs)

122. 'Dressing up'
Betty Bertrand (2.5hrs)

123. Small Person
Valerie Horner

124. Mr and Mrs Wood
Anne Boyle (45hrs)

125. Mela Poster
Jackie Moore (3hrs)

126. Kosovan Refugees
Margaret Clark (17hrs)

127. Trevor Griffiths
Anne Boyle (50hrs)

128. Rosie Kearton
Rose Kearton (9hrs)

129. Bonfire Night 1
June Hardy (4hrs)

130. Bonfire Night 2
June Hardy (4hrs)

131. Boy with Top Hat
Susan Lawton (8hrs)

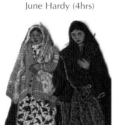

132. Two Asian Ladies
Ann Brown

133. Arshima
Ayesha Dost

134. Kate
Valerie Kent

135. Three Little Maids
Sallie Lindley (150hrs)

136. Yorkshire Water
Judy Poole

137. St Martin's Hospice
Betty Laycock

138. Drop the Debt
Jackie Baron & J. Taylor (46hrs)

139. Mela Food Stalls
Janet Carding (30hrs)

140. Foyle & Kirk
Betty Bertrand

141. Meanwood Farm
Betty Laycock

142. Beacon
Jenny McLean (1hr)

143. Wheatfield's Hospice
Joyce James (50hrs)

144. Hen
Laura Hebden (2.25hrs)

145. Traveller's Caravan
Anne Boyle (60hrs)

146. Garden Shed
Barbara Walker (5hrs)

147. Allotments
J.Taylor & E.Thackrah

148. 'Child's Place' Group
Margaret Milne (20hrs)

149. Traveller
Julia Cooper

150. Road
Elizabeth Thackrah (35.5hrs)

151. Trees
Margaret Kenny

152. Hale-Bopp
Elizabeth Thackrah (2hrs)

153. 'Child's Place' Bus
Joan Holah (14hrs)

154. Skippko
Val Gomersall

155. HSBC
Sally Walton (10hrs)

156. Barbara Walker

157. Lincoln Green
Hilary Thurlow

158. John Speed Memorial
Janet Taylor (10hrs)

159. Intake School
Janet Taylor (12hrs)

160. 'Caring Together"
Ena Dunn (10hrs)

161. Signers at Swarthmore
Barbara Hebden(77hrs)

162. Swarthmore Board
Joyce James (25hrs)

163. Gloria (T'ai Chi)
Ena Dunn

164. Valorie Patillo
Val Gomersall

165. Radiant Health Flag
Mary T Sanders

166. Jason Chan
Sheila Slater (12hrs)

167. Elaine McRorie
Val Gomersall

168. Victor Spence
Val Gomersall (20hrs)

169. Doran
Janet Taylor

170. Youth at Risk
Joyce Maynard (5hrs)
171. Arcadia Group

172. Community Policemen
Mary Sanders

173. Big Issue Seller
Dorothy Wrench (5hrs)

174. Man with Flute
Gill Cook

175. Leeds Amateur Operatics
Barbara Walker (1hr)

176. Pat from Armley Mills
Claire Wildman

177. Methodist Homes
Judith Jackson (3hrs)

178. Man in Waistcoat
Ena Dunn

179. Babies' Welcome
Anne Boyle (12hrs)

180. Mother & Child
Archana Singh

181. Hilary & Jonathan
Renee Silverman (20hrs)

182. Millennium Festival Logo
Mary Sanders (10hrs)

183. Alan Titchmarsh
Myra Turner (4hrs)

184. Tuesday Luncheon Club
Eileen Wilson (100hrs)

185. Lady Diana
Jackie Ford

186. BPW Yorkshire
Joyce James

187. Girl with Camera
Helen Sedgewick (8hrs)

188. 'Black Elders" Decorator
Evi Malm (15hrs)

The processes of research, discussion and fund-raising were the most time-consuming elements on all panels but on this panel more than most. Over 1,000 community groups were approached by letter and hundreds more by word of mouth through the volunteer network.

Many volunteers, Ruth Fowler for example, did wonderful work in persuading groups they knew to take the opportunity to be portrayed on this panel representing the Spirit of Community. Having successfully involved the Girls' Brigade she felt bold enough to tackle the Boys. Paula Convy, who worked with the project part-time as Office Manager from 1998-2000, also made and nurtured contacts, bringing in the Child Place Group who collect children from school and look after them until parents finish work. Her son James is standing beside the van on the final piece (153).

Other part-time consultants were brought in specifically to support the work of liaising with approximately 300 different groups and individuals. Penny Stephenson was with the Tapestry for 9 months and during this period co-ordinated the mailings, follow-up and data-base creation. Jan Wells, free-lance photographer and video maker, worked with many individuals and groups to produce images to represent themselves authentically. The excellent and lively images of Louise Read, the Mela Festival, Lincoln Green Youth Centre, the

Vaisakhi Festival, the Travellers' Association and the Chapel Allerton Allotments were all selected from Jan's work.

Penny was able to open up the opportunity for many groups and individuals to take part in creating *Community Spirit* by successfully applying for a Millennium Festival Award. Groups such as Caring Together, Latin American Women's Association, Youth at Risk, The Black Elders, Latch, The Big Issue and Wheatfields Hospice could now be included.

The award from the Millennium Festival Fund, together with a smaller but still very useful sum from the Leeds City Council 'Community Chest', took some of the pressure off the project's fund-raisers and enabled everyone who was interested to be included.

Earlier in the life of this panel when the future for it looked bleak, the co-founder of the Radiant Health Foundation, Jason Chan, who was Kate's Tai Chi teacher, agreed to perform his art at an evening fund-raiser. He was aiming to raise at least £1,000 to contribute to the panel and his

23.
Boy from Lincoln Green
Barbara Hebden (5hrs)

100.
Matron Jean Walker
Val Gomersall

153.
'Child's Place' Bus
Joan Holah (14hrs)

115.
Girls at Lincoln Green
Hilary Thurlow (18hrs)

94.
Camaraman & boy
Jackie Ford (8hrs)

6.
Bharata Natyam Dance
Victoria Russell (35hrs)

The Spice of Leeds

CHAPELTOWN & HAREHILLS
URBAN INITIATIVE

189.
The Spice of Leeds
Celia Charnley (20hrs)
Not used on the panel.

20.
Chinese Dragron
Renee Silverman
(200hrs)

students and volunteers from the project came from far and wide with their families and friends. Skills and services, including reflexology, energy work, acupuncture, feng-shui and tai chi lessons were ably and flamboyantly auctioned by Mirella Rugolotto (of Co-ventures, sponsors on the Civic Pride panel). A good time was had by all and £2,900 was raised for the panel.

There was a huge amount of support but Rosie Kearton and Kate still needed to work full time on the all-consuming task of meetings, telephone conversations, etc. There were then months of follow up to ensure that the logos, buildings, people etc on this and the *Education* panel were used in accordance with groups wishes. Rosie appears on both panels - here as a participant in a pioneering New Working Ways course.

Often the people concerned did not possess photos and if they did, the quality was not clear or bright enough to do them justice! In such cases a photographer, often Paul Wilkinson or Martin Banks, was hired to attend and record an event and if no one else was available, Kate would get the job. Sometimes it was impossible to have a specific photograph taken within the deadline so Barbara would literally pick up the pieces - using parts of photographs that were clear, cannibalising and re-jigging hundreds of images and spending many thousands of hours in the process. She was given a brilliant picture of some dancers, one of them being slightly obscured by a dustbin. When she returned it the bin was missing, as well as the posterior of another dancer who had bent down at the wrong moment and no-one had noticed. Barbara was, at the eleventh hour, persuaded to be included (back view only!) where a customer was needed to use the cashpoint at the Chapel Allerton Branch of the HSBC bank. Despite her persistence in getting embroiderers to record their names against work this one eludes her. It seems to have been done in the style of Sandra Sutton's accordion player but there is no trace of her address to check this.

As always the design metamorphosed according to the thousands of conversations and ideas. Many groups who were initially approached and included in the design were not, for one reason or another, embroidered. Perhaps a key person to approve the design was not available at the last deadline or a planned photo shoot could not happen due to bad weather or illness or the volunteer was unable to complete the embroidery in time. Some projects literally expanded in the making so that others were inevitably pushed out.

The main principles of the design held fast more or less throughout - a bonfire in the distance with fireworks against the night sky and a procession inspired by the wondrous festival originating in Chapeltown (now called the Leeds Festival which happens every August Bank Holiday) winding from the top of the panel to the foreground. On either side of the road are 'audiences' made up of groups and individuals; to the right those situated in more urban environments; to the left more rural.

Resident road and tree experts were in demand with Elizabeth Thackrah creating yards of densely machine stitched road. This was worked from many detailed shots of gravel paths and took into account in the stitching of the texture the need to create an illusion of distance. Margaret Kenny excelled herself creating dozens of bushes and trees of varying sizes. These were excellent visual aids when attempting

to bring all the sections together. The trees which could not be used on this panel were easily transplanted onto *Faith in Leeds.*

Unlike *Civic Pride* the majority of the embroidered people are real. Most of the projects started as photographic images giving many of the volunteers more confidence to work on them. Many were photographed for the Tapestry as organisations and the individuals have not yet been identified. Others were included because of their individual contribution to community projects. Danny Freeman (77) for instance has spent many years outside Marks & Spencer singing and raising money for charities and Joan Walker was Matron at St Mary's Maternity Hospital. Joan stitched the embroidery of herself and her patient onto the panel. Mr Baron was one of the campaigners for the building of Leeds Playhouse.

The staff at Armley Mills are represented (72, 176). As one of them, Pat Lynch, provided the image of the Morris Dancers (10), she appears twice on the panel. When the project moved from there to Holy Trinity two of the cafe staff there were asked if they would like to

77.
Danny Freeman
Sheila Exley

72.
Staff from Armley Mills
Claire Wildman

111.
*Mr Baron &
Grandchild*
Mrs Baron

10.
Morris Dancers
Betty Bertrand (30hrs)

92.
Kate & Betty
Betty Bertrand

133.
Arshima
Ayesha Dost

68.
Audrey Pidgeon
Joan Holah (14hrs)

109.
Veronica & her dad
Veronica Dore

appear on the panel (66,67) and also the Community Policemen from that beat (172). Both policemen have a full complement of legs in real life. Often people had to have limbs chopped off to prevent too much bulk on the final piece.

On many of the panels there is at least one of the embroiderers. In this case we have the late Audrey Pidgeon (68), a lovely lady who kept everyone amused at workshops. It is a great tribute to her that after she died and the fifteen panels were on display at Harewood, her relatives, friends and neighbors all came to check the database to make sure she had been included. Kate and Betty are seen here (92) penny pinching. Holy Trinity was so close to the Queen's Hotel that for one event they manhandled *Transport* along Boar Lane. Veronica Dore, one of the volunteers (109) hand embroidered the piece of herself with her Dad.

Ayesha Dost, with her daughter, hand embroidered her self-portrait but also took away other projects to be embroidered in the northern Indian state of Uttar Pradesh. The principal

stitch used is Aari, though other stitches included Zardozi, Sitara, Badla, French knots, Challa work, Chamki work and Tilla work. The majority doing this work are Muslim men and most of the pieces for Leeds Tapestry were done by Zuber Mohammed and his team. They transfer the pattern to the fabric by taking a tracing, covering it with a mixture of kerosene and chalk then with a pin pricking along the lines of the pattern through to the fabric. These tiny holes are then highlighted with chalk and form the outline of the pattern on the fabric. The fabric is framed and the artisan sits on the floor to work. The thread is held in one hand under the fabric and a hooked needle passed through from the top. Aari work resembles a fine chain stitch and in the finished work the background fabric should not be visible. The piece on this panel (133) has the word *Arshima* on it, meaning *the heavenly one*, inscribed in different Indian languages: Urdu, Hindi, Gujarati, Bengali and Punjabi

Transferring images to fabric using the computer and printer was not without problems. When the Lottery equipment first arrived many tests were carried out printing straight onto the fabric. Different weights of fabric were glued to paper and fed through the ink jet printer with varying results. The ink was not colour fast but it was felt that, as the whole panel was not going to be washed, it was acceptable. Kate was not reckoning on some of the embroiderers steam ironing their finished works. Joyce James embroidered Wheatfields Hospice (143) highlighting the flowers in the foreground with french knots and single chain stitch, and then pressed it. The result was a happy accident. The colours began to run on the background print giving the final piece a beautiful subdued effect.

Phase Two was to use T-shirt transfer paper and experiments were done with different makes of paper ironed on to different weights of cotton, silk and polyester fabrics. Transfer papers make fabric a lot stiffer and the hand embroiderers had problems getting their needles through closely woven materials. There was almost a mutiny when the manufacturer of the chosen paper introduced a new and improved product. It may have been fine for decorating T-shirts but it turned embroidery fabrics into sail cloth. Renee

Silverman spent hours hand stitching her daughter-in-law and grandson (181). She ironed it when finished and the face turned into a shrivelled prune. Fortunately Renee had by this time become one of the volunteers who printed the images, so she made another face and transplanted it onto the original, lengthening the hair and heightening the collar to cover the join.

The unveiling in October 2000 was all set to be one of the most glorious - Sylvia and Rosie had worked together with Railtrack and the Queen's Hotel to produce an impressive event. It was to begin with the unveiling of the completed panel in the Northern Concourse of the City Station, where several other panels were already on display. Irish and Asian musicians and dancers would entertain the crowds and all volunteers and those groups and individuals who had participated in the panels were invited. Sponsors and ticket holders would then assemble for a multi-cultural buffet in the Queen's Hotel where an exhibition of work in progress was assembled for all to see. All this was to be covered by TV and local press to give much needed publicity. Unfortunately the day selected was the terrible day of the Hatfield crash. Obviously all Railtrack staff were needed elsewhere and the Concourse had to be cleared. The Queen's Hotel were very responsive to the emergency and set up the whole event in their ballroom, where the launch continued although with dampened spirits.

190.
Latch House
Vivienne Brown (10hrs)

181.
Hilary & Jonathon
Renee Silverman
(20hrs)

143.
Wheatfield's Hospice
Joyce James (50hrs)

1. Joan's Grandchildren
Joan Holah (12hrs)

2. Skater
Dorothy Wrench (3hrs)

3. Skater
Dorothy Wrench (3hrs)

4. Skater
Dorothy Wrench (3hrs)

5. Skater
Dorothy Wrench (3hrs)

6. Skater
Dorothy Wrench (3hrs)

7. Albert Johanneson
Muriel Gabbitas

8. Jack Charlton
Eileen Page & J. Holah

9. Darren Gough
Margaret Clark

10. Lucas Radabe
Dorothy Wrench (4hrs)

11. David Batty
Dorothy Wrench (4hrs)

12. Alan Smith
Dorothy Wrench (4hrs)

13. Olivier Dacourt
Dorothy Wrench (4hrs)

14. Eirik Bakke
Dorothy Wrench (4hrs)

15. Cyclists
Cynthia Jackson

16. George Duncan
Betty Bertrand

17. Moor Allerton Golf
Club
Joan Holah (40hrs)

18. Mrs Moody
Carol Marshall

19. Carnegie College
Joan Holah (12hrs)

20. John Charles
Janet Carding (42hrs)

21. Beryl Burton
Anne Boyle

22. Nick Gale (41hrs)
A. Brown & E. Thackrah

23. Mick Hill
Janet Taylor (7hrs)

24. Angie Hulley
Joan Holah

25. Gymnasts
Barbara Walker (5hrs)

26. Intake Skateboarders
Betty Bertrand

27. Free Fall
Gill Cook

28. Billy Bremner
Muriel Gabbitas (42hrs)

29. Rugby Players
Pat Potton

30. British Judo Association
Joyce James (5hrs)

31. Debbie Dunn
M. Whaley (4hrs)

32. Yorkshire Shield
Joan Holah (8hrs)

33. Yorkshire Shield
Audrey Pidgeon

34. Bramley Rugby Shield
Ann Wheatley

35. Cycle Race
Janet Taylor (10hrs)

36. Alan Smith
Jackie Ford

37. Leeds United F.C.
Joyce Maynard

38. Leeds Football Stadium
Janet Taylor (7hrs)

39. Rugby Stadium
Kathryn Vincent

40. Ice Skater
Renee Silverman

41. Leeds Golf Club
Barbara Walker (5hrs)

42. Leeds Golf Club
Joan Langfield (20hrs)

43. Alwoodley Golf Club
Margaret Turnbull (200hrs)

44. Leeds Rhinos
Brenda Archer (4hrs)

45. Disability Sports
Beryl Smith (8hrs)

46. Wheelchair Racing
Sallie Lindley

47. Sporting Life
Maureen Carr

48. Yorkshire Electricity
Joyce James

49. Sports Aid Foundation
Joyce Maynard

50. Sports Council
Val Gomersall

51. Leeds Albion Cycling Club
Lesley Dove

52. Chapel Allerton Tennis
Maureen Carr

53. Len Hutton
Merel Jackson (14hrs)

54. Headingley Ground
Janet Taylor (12hrs)

55. The Village
Janet Carding

56. Sport for All
Pat Potton (14hrs)

57. Girl in Pool
Renee Silverman

58. Ann Hardy
Janet Carding (6hrs)

59. Leeds Marathon
Janet Carding (4hrs)

60. Adrian Moorhouse
Barbara Gray (65hrs)

61. Leeds Swimming Club
Joan Holah (3hrs)

62. Bowling Alley
Val Gomersall

63. Football Game
Cynthia Jackson

64. Hilton Gym
Val Gomersall

65. South Leeds Stadium
Joan Holah (150hrs)

66. 'Welcome to Leeds'
Denise Teed (18hrs)

67. Bouncy Castle
Val Gomersall

68. Football
Janet Taylor (2hrs)

69. Golf Balls
Betty Bertrand

70. Tennis Ball
Janet Taylor (2hrs)

Bowling Alley in detail

As with the *Local Faces* panel, the consultation for this panel was started early. The general public, volunteers and, since the majority of the embroiderers were women, their spouses were dragged into the conversations too. Spouses involved included those with sporting connections like Maureen's husband Neville Carr of Chapel Allerton Lawn Tennis and Squash Club and Lesley Dove's husband Robin, whose historical knowledge and collection of Very Useful Books was unsurpassed (he provided images for 18, 32,33,34,51,71). More formal gatherings of information were held with the Regional Sports Council and several Leeds City Council sports officers, one in the company of the Lord Mayor, Councillor Peggy White, herself a keen sportswoman.

Again, funding was very hard to come by and in over seven years of trying we raised less than 50% of the estimated cost of producing the panel. Many sections were sponsored through volunteers' efforts. Neville Carr secured funds on behalf of the CALTSC and Maureen embroidered the resulting design (52). This was our first and only funding for this panel for many years.

Betty Bertrand, a keen golfer, interested her own club, Moortown, and hand-embroidered the design showing George Duncan in front of the clubhouse so beautifully and to such acclaim from her fellow

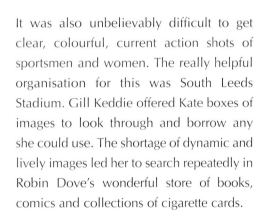

golfers that she made a second piece which is now framed and hung in the clubhouse. Her efforts also brought on board the other golf clubs: Moor Allerton, Leeds, and Alwoodley.

Jenny Williams and Shirley Gale persuaded both the Village Leisure Club (55) and the British Judo Association to make donations to have their logos represented on the panel. Shirley's son Nick (22), an asthmatic from being a child, who against all odds became British Judo Champion, is portrayed admirably through Ann Brown's combined strengths of drawing and hand embroidery. The image is taken from a pharmacy company's advert for an asthma drug. The rest of the sponsors were the result of years of sheer persistence on Sylvia's part.

It was also unbelievably difficult to get clear, colourful, current action shots of sportsmen and women. The really helpful organisation for this was South Leeds Stadium. Gill Keddie offered Kate boxes of images to look through and borrow any she could use. The shortage of dynamic and lively images led her to search repeatedly in Robin Dove's wonderful store of books, comics and collections of cigarette cards.

The idea of presenting the sports images as the front page of a colourful comic newspaper appealed to Kate, partly to get across the lively participatory nature of *Sporting Life*. For similar reasons she was very keen to get young people – especially graffiti 'artists' involved in the designing of this panel. The Leeds TEC (Technical Education Council), through Norah Keaney, supported this through an Artist's Residency at Intake High School and Art College. Kate spent a day a week at the college for several months working with Mike Jolly, Head of

67.
Bouncy Castle
Val Gomersall

27.
Free Fall
Gill Cook

16.
George Duncan
Betty Bertrand

63.
Football Game
Cythnia Jackson

40.
Ice Skater
Renee Silverman

25.
Gymnasts
Barbara Walker (5hrs)

71.
R Menzel
J Kirk (51.5hrs)

Art, in setting up a studio in the sixth form classroom. Many students were involved (Angela Lambert, Leon Barham, Lisa Dickinson, Natalie Gains, Tana Massey and Gemma Stocks) in collaborative design for the Tapestry. The graffiti-style logo, the cartoon rugby players, the gymnasts, skateboarders and Leeds Stadium all came out of this process. The ice skater was spotted in the current college newsletter and brilliantly interpreted by Renee Silverman, whose capacity for challenge and experiment is still growing.

Kathryn Vincent, a senior teacher at the college, who ferried Kate to and fro each week, became enthusiastic enough about the project to spend many hours stitching the Rhinos ground and stand. This was charted on the computer by Peter Cowgill with very visually dynamic results.

Another design strategy used to bring life to this panel was to have people, parts of people, badges and balls jumping out of the picture rectangles. Also the background net and colour was manipulated to bring a sense of movement to the whole. This in itself was no easy task. Having tried both drawing and photographing different nets, fiddling and stretching the images on the computer to no avail, Kate eventually achieved the desired result by photocopying borrowed nets – just laying the net over the photocopier – and enlarging, reducing and piecing together, patching in drawing where necessary.

Kate was thrilled when Wendy, the print technician at Leeds College of Art, said that she and her colleagues would be able to screenprint both the net and the blended Leeds United colours in the background.

This involved yet another textile technique and was a most excellent method to show the quality of the net without it becoming too dominant. Leeds College of Art, through Garry Barker's outreach work, also supported textile technique workshops, both at Armley Mills and at Holy Trinity Church over a period of three years, providing a much appreciated life-line when the project was at its lowest ebb. Kate was delighted to acknowledge this support from the College by including their 'mosaic' logo in the border of *Education*.

Many of the people included were nominated by guests at fund raising events where the cartoon of the panel was on display. One or two like Len Hutton and John Charles were also put forward for *Local Faces*. We apologise for the all too brief biographies following but hope it is sufficient to indicate why people were selected.

Albert Johanneson was the first black player to appear in an FA Cup Final at Wembley, for Leeds against Liverpool, in 1965. He left the club in 1970 to join York City but after a brief return to his native South Africa he came back to Leeds. Despite help from many friends to cure his drink problem he died alone in 1995.

Jack Charlton (b 1935), a Geordie, joined Leeds in 1950 and was one of the team in Revie's glory years, winning the FA Cup in 1972. Charlton himself was Footballer of the Year in 1967. John Charles (b1931) was signed for Leeds on his sixteenth birthday and stayed with the team for about ten years. Known as the *Gentle Giant* he is said by many to be Leeds greatest player outside the Revie era. Billy Bremner, another of the old favourites, as Captain lead the team to two league championships, an FA Cup win and two Inter-Cities Fairs Cups. Five current players were needed to set the scene for the East Stand (built for the start of the 1993-4 season) drawn by one of the pupils at Intake High School. Chosen by Robin Walker, then aged 13, they are Lucas Radabe (former Captain and still figure head), David Batty (a legend and liked by most fans), Alan Smith (Leeds born and bred and one of the few locals to have a regular place), Olivier Dacourt (a new signing at the time but impressive) and Bakke (his favourite player now and then). Talking about it three years later with the embroiderer, both Robin and Dorothy agreed it was a good choice, all were still playing for Leeds.

The County Cricket Ground at Headingley opened in 1888 with its first test match

held in 1899 was machine embroidered by Janet Taylor. The spectators here witnessed Don Bradman's 300 runs in one day at a test match and Geoff Boycott's one-hundreth hundred. Sir Len Hutton (53), another high scorer, was chosen to use the nets at Headingley when he was only 13 and his success continued. In 1934 he scored the first of 129 centuries for county and country and his record 364 runs in a test in 1938 wasn't beaten for decades. Darren Gough (b1970) appears as one of the more recent players. He made his first class debut at the age of nineteen and was Wisden Cricketer of the Year in 1999. Lord Hawke (1860-1938) on the Yorkshire Shield (32) may be less well known nowadays but he was Yorkshire captain for 28 years.

Beryl Burton (1937-1996) was chosen for the panel by the Yorkshire Road Cycling Club. Beryl was born in Morley and was virtually unbeaten on the track and in road trails in the UK for 25 years. Wheeled sports are also represented by the Leeds Albion Cycling Club badge hand sewn and built up in layers by Leslie Dove and by wheelchair racing, one of the disability sports events entered in the 2002 Commonwealth games.

Mick Hill (b1964), a javelin thrower was not only born in Leeds but also went to Carnegie College in the city and was consistently in the world's top ten between 1987 and 1998. Finally Adrian Moorhouse from Bingley who trained at Leeds as a school boy and went on to win Olympic Gold at breaststroke in the Seoul Olympics

Sporting Life was one of the easiest panels to put together. It just seemed to happen in amongst all the others without any struggle.

12.
Alan Smith
Dorothy Wrench (4hrs)

21.
Beryl Burton
Anne Boyle

23.
Mick Hill
Janet Taylor (7hrs)

54.
Headingley Ground
Janet Taylor (12hrs)

1. Beetle

2. Dragonfly sample
Hilary Thurlow

3. Dragonfly sample
Margaret Foxcroft

4. Meanwood Farm Animals
Valerie Horner (12hrs)

5. Frog
Ena Dunn (22hrs)

6. Aireborough Shield
Margaret Clark (29hrs)

7. Environmental Health
Beryl Smith (38.5hrs)

8. Yorkshire Environmental
Rosie Kearton

9. Eye on the Aire
Joan Holah (110hrs)

10. Carl Bro Group
Mary Sanders

11. Rivercare
Joan Holah (80hrs)

12. Meanwood Valley Farm
Betty Bertrand

13. Geofabrics
Gill Cook

14. Granary Wharf
Jan Brown

15. Environment Agency
Eileen Wilson

16. Meanwood Farm Sign
Valerie Horner (5hrs)
17. Working for the Environment
Joyce Maynard (3hrs)

18. British Waterways
Mary Sanders

19. Geofabrics (parts)
Gill Cook

Environment City
CREATING A SUSTAINABLE FUTURE

In 1994 when the *West Riding Rag Ruggers* and their chair, Isabel Waterhouse, expressed their enthusiasm for taking part in producing one of the panels, it was obvious that *Environment City* was the one. The process of cutting discarded fabric into strips and then hooking or prodding them into canvas or hessian to make rugs was perfectly in keeping with the current ideas of re-cycling and sustainability. This process was widely used by families during the war years and throughout the Industrial Revolution. Leeds City Council had won the 'Environment City' award in 1993 so the title was already chosen for us.

After these effortless decisions the struggle started. Everyone was interested in the idea, everyone wanted to talk and share their points of view about what should go into the panel – but no-one had any funds or resources to spare. Ethics became involved. Was it acceptable to seek sponsorship from the huge chemical firms who had money and expressed an interest in 'cleaning up' their professions but who still seemed to be adding to the pollution of our waterways?

Sue Reddington, Director of Meanwood Valley Urban Farm, was the first sponsor for this panel. Long before there was any design to see she put her faith in the Tapestry by persuading one of the project's sponsors to put in some extra funds to have the Farm represented on this panel. In appreciation of Sue's support not only for this panel but the whole project – her advice, moral support, enthusiasm and the sharing of many of her contacts – her great work at the Urban Farm was acknowledged on the *Community Spirit* panel.

Eric Cowin (a long term supporter of the Tapestry project) also gave all the financial and other help he could. Through *Eye on the Aire* he commissioned a portrait of the charity's co-founder Susan Marsden, again before the design was even started. The intention was to include her on the *Environment City* panel but as the designs emerged it was obvious that her rightful place was on *Local Faces*.

Eric and *Eye on the Aire* also provided other boosts to morale and funding. In September 1998 when Michael Meacher, Minister of the Environment, was invited to one of their events Eric asked if the Tapestry would like to exhibit the four completed panels, *Pro Rege et Lege*, *Money Works*, *Enterprise* and *Civic Pride*. The event was held at the Innovation Centre in The Calls where the panels would be seen by the visiting politician. The Minister was obviously bowled over by what he saw of the panels and said it was the most vibrant example of contemporary embroidery he had seen. He added that

2.
Dragonfly
Hilary Thurlow

9.
Eye on the Aire
Joan Holah (110hrs)

14.
Granary Wharf
Jan Brown

Dentdale
Christine Pitchfork (11hrs)
Not used on the panel.

Scarecrow Sample
Margaret Kenny

Leeds City Council "must be over the moon" to have the Tapestry being created in its midst. Like us, he saw the enormous public relations value in the image of citizens creating their own city stitch by stitch. We did not, of course, disillusion him but basked in the warmth of his response for several months. His well-chosen reference to the Tapestry in his speech about *Eye on the Aire* and the work being done on the Environment enlisted many more company sponsors, including people we had been courting for years. This was the kind of support most needed and was lacking. Public statements of the project's value to the city and its citizens, throughout the ten years of making, could have re-vitalised the process of participation, bringing in the people, the photos, the funds which were so needed. From the first sponsor in 1994 to the last in 2001 (the Leeds Environment City Partnership), less than 50% of the financial target was reached for this panel.

From the hundreds of conversations it was apparent that the content of the panel would be the process of environmental degradation, the massive pollution of the 'Air above and the Aire below' and the gradual awareness and cleaning up processes. Kate wanted somehow to show 'England's Green and Pleasant Land' – its despoiling and its potential recovery, including the contributions to this made by the sponsors, in one visually unified compelling image.

Kate saw an 1893 engraving of a bird's eye view of the River Aire, with the city growing and sprouting mill chimneys alongside it,

and knew she had found the vehicle needed to carry these ideas. The process of enlarging and re-drawing was lengthy. The first stage was to square up the rather faded print and enlarge it freehand to the biggest size which would fit on the drawing board (A2). This process took five days, after which it was enlarged in sections to the full panel size using a photocopier. At this point a small sample of the enlarged version was sent to Diane West (the new chair of West Riding Ruggers) and Margaret Kenny to see if the group (still interested after all these years!) could manage to 'hook' so finely. Whilst they were both keen and enthusiastic in the workshop it was later reported that Diane's response to the daunting task was unprintable.

Margaret produced the first samples and some wonderfully fine canvas for the panel. Both looked ideal but then came the problem of transposing the map to canvas. What was needed was an enormous light table such as those used by architects and planners. Weeks of searching revealed none; such equipment seems to have been abandoned in favour of computers. Fortunately Janet Taylor, who had studied at Bretton Hall College and knew there was one there, organised for Kate and herself to use it and after many back-breaking days and dozens of felt tip pens the canvas was ready to hand over to the Ruggers.

A colour chart and plan of spaces to leave blank for embroidered insertions was provided for the team. The bottom third of the image was to look bright, green and abundant moving

upwards gradually becoming darker, smoky and oppressive with the top section showing a vision of industrial and natural resources co-existing happily and creating a sustainable future. The colour changes of bricks, tiles, greenery and river were beautiful and very subtle and Kate felt they may be a stretch for the technique of rugging.

A year later, when Kate saw the finished product, she was amazed not only at the speed of execution but also by the quality of the work. Diane as chairwoman and Margaret as co-ordinator of colour had turned the panel into one of the most visually satisfying of them all. The workers on the ragrugging section were Margaret Kenny, Diane West, Veronica Metcalfe, Trudy Dracup, Penny Godfrey, Marjorie Hopkinson, Isobel Waterhouse, Mary Lee, Nancy Hartby, Mick Trott, Elaine Foster, Renee Cole and Jennifer Clough. The delightful wildlife; frog, beetle and dragonflies were made in or inspired by workshops given by Sarah Hodgson and Hilary Thurlow. Margaret Foxcroft and Janet Taylor made two of the dragonflies.

Breakdowns occur in the best organised projects and this was no exception. Kate recalls one decision about this panel that she later regretted. The Ruggers asked to have the completed panel as part of their exhibition at the Bradford Industrial Museum, where much of the group work had been done. Kate was so appreciative of their incredible work that she agreed. The timing of their event could not have been worse as it was right in the middle of the frantic weeks just before the exhibition opened at Harewood. Kate says it was not because of the extra work and cost entailed, but because miscommunications and

frayed nerves between all the people involved: museum staff, handlers and transporters, volunteers and herself, led to a breakdown in

Working on the panel.

what she thought was a great relationship with the group. A relationship where vision, determination, hours of skilful labour and love had come together to create an artwork which none of the individuals could have created alone. Thankfully the piece itself, unmarred by all the upset, remains a credit to all the Ruggers and to the volunteers who embroidered the uniquely beautiful inserts.

11.
Rivercare
Joan Holah (80hrs)

It took brute strength and heavy industrial staplers to stretch the finished canvas onto the frame before attaching the inserts and the volunteers who achieved this feat also deserve a mention. There were problems during the rugging with the canvas stretching disproportionately according to the varied 'hooking' techniques of the volunteers. The whole canvas had stretched lengthways about six inches, as had the *Picture of Health* panel, but in this case the extra could not be gathered up by extra padding. Some of the design at the bottom was lost and the sponsor sections had to be rearranged. Also the gaps carefully positioned to take the embroideries changed upwards and sideways so after the sections had been attached Margaret and Diane had to come back and fill in the gaps.

Sample of rag rugging.
Margaret Kenny

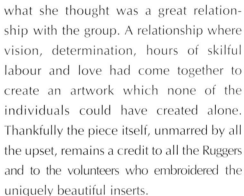

1. 1840 Map
Ann Wheatley

2. 1770 Map
Jan Brown

3. 1900s Map
Ann Wheatley

4. Shield with Lamb
June Stockwell

5. Leeds Coat of Arms
Beryl Smith (40hrs)

6. Cossin's Map
Joan Holah (100hrs)

7. Rack and Pinion Loco
Lesley Dove

8. Leeds Transport Map
Joan Holah (100hrs)

9. Leeds Inner Loop
Joan Holah (100hrs)

10. Vauxhall Calibra
Renee Davidson (50hrs)

11. Air UK
Audrey Pidgeon

12. Ledgard Bus
Eileen Wilson (12hrs)

13. Blackburn Monoplane
Audrey Pidgeon (20hrs)

14. Royal Mail Van
Godfrey Harland (40hrs)

15. Metro Hotline
Barbara Gray (5hrs)

16. Metro Logo
Barbara Walker (1hr)

17. Metro Post
B.M. Fox

18. Metro Bus Station
Joan Holah

19. 1939 Vauxhall
Janet Carding

20. Burton's Van
Barbara Gray (6hrs)

21. Coal Barge
Merel Jackson (7hrs)

22. Kirkstall/Roundhay Tram

23. 'Stylo' Tram
Eileen Wilson (12hrs)

24. 'Bovril' Tram
Eileen Wilson

25. 'The City of Leeds'
Mary Mawson (63.5hrs)

26. First Bus by Barbara
Walker (1hr)
27. Northern Spirit by Joyce
James

28. GNER Coaster
Eileen Wilson

29. Leeds/Bradford Airport
Lizzie Ingle & G. Harland

30. Albert Farnell
Joan Holah

31. Classic Cars
Betty Laycock

32. Archbold Lorry
Pat Andrews

33. Station Concourse
Godfrey Harland (28hrs)

34. X35 Rider Bus
Olwen Poulter (15hrs)

35. Wallace Arnold
Godfrey Harland (20hrs)

36. BR Train 321903
Mary Smith (10hrs)

37. Virgin Train
Godfrey Harland (19hrs)

38. Midland Mainline
Joyce James

39. Express Train 158740
Eileen Wilson

40. Train
Jan Brown (60hrs)

42. Kate's Hand
Jackie Ford (6hrs)

41. Cyclist
Joan Holah (5hrs)

43. Loop Sign
Joan Holah (13hrs)

44. Delivery Bike
Marion Cole, Brian and Merel Jackson

45. Cycle Path
Joan Holah (13hrs)

31.
Classic Cars
Betty Laycock

12.
Ledgard Bus
Eileen Wilson (12hrs)

The consultation process usually starts very casually as it did with this panel. Questions were dropped into conversations about other Tapestry topics and in early 1995 the first visual items were pinned onto a panel sized board designated *Transport*.

Whilst at Armley Mills Museum Kate asked Eric Marshall to make sufficient full size pin boards for each of the panels we still had to produce. Eric did all the joinery work throughout the ten-year project apart from framing the panels. Unfortunately, due to lack of space, the twelve boards had to be stacked on top of each other. They were interspersed with several timber frames with cotton backcloths stretched over them - panels under construction. The boards and frames were regularly juggled around so the ones needed were at the front.

Eileen Wilson's husband Donald was very helpful on this panel, transport being a lifelong hobby of his. He provided books, book titles, photos, slides and other useful information. The staff at Armley Mills and visitors to the Museum added many other items to the board.

Maps were introduced to illustrate the development of Leeds from hamlet to town and its growth since it became a city in 1893. This idea of using maps, to show the expansion of the transport networks through the centuries, originated with the *In the Beginning* panel which was to have used this theme. Kate had already been collecting copies of the beautiful early maps of the city and the design for this panel started to take shape when she found references to the Middleton Railway.

The developing concept for *On the Move* was of historic maps, stained, monochromatic and suitably 'aged', with time marching on and upwards on the panel. This would culminate in a full-colour city map showing up-to-the-minute transport changes at the beginning of the year 2000.

By the time the full scale cartoon of the panel was put together there were several small sections of embroidered *Transport* items that did not quite fit. 'Smeaton's Engine', 'The Mallard', 'Mousell Bros', the 'tram ticket', trams, steam engines and barges were all originally embroidered for the *Transport* panel. Luckily they all fitted admirably into *Pins and Needles*. All that is except the splendid barge embroidered by Pauline Clayden. Kate was sure that it would find a home on either *Environment City* or *Pins and Needles* but it was not to be. Sometimes she would stand in front of

2.
1770 Map
Jan Brown

5.
Leeds Coat of Arms
Beryl Smith (40hrs)

Narrow Boat's Butty
Pauline Clayden
Not used on the panel.

a panel design for most of the day, moving and re-pinning sections until her fingers were sore, attempting to make a square peg fit into a round hole. Disappointingly this was one time when her efforts failed, so this piece lies in a box with others which suffered the same fate, awaiting a new life in the *Serendipity* panel. All that is needed is a creative soul with enough energy to design and co-ordinate such a panel for all the 'homeless' embroideries.

Sometimes sponsors themselves gave considerable help in fund-raising. During the refurbishment of the Northern Concourse of Leeds City Station, Gordon Carey of Carey Jones Architects had made a proposal that the completed Tapestry be displayed down the centre of the Concourse. Railtrack were keen on the idea and talks proceeded with the Tapestry Board of Trustees over many years and changes of management finally resulting in a huge mobile display being made. This case is capable of holding eight panels and is currently situated in the Concourse. During this period various Railtrack staff members

helped to co-ordinate the funding and representation of all the rail networks using Leeds Station. This made an enormous difference both to the success of these negotiations and to the availablity of photographs of new livery and logos.

38.
Midland Mainline
Joyce James

Sonia Kenson of Metro (WYPTE) was also incredibly supportive over the years; initially in sponsoring the representation of Metro on *Transport*, *Community Spirit*, and *Enterprise* panels. She also joined us in identifying and following up potential sponsors amongst her colleagues and at times of greatest crisis came up trumps by, for example, agreeing an advance payment on postcards of *Transport* when we were virtually out of funds!

25.
'The City of Leeds'
Mary Mawson (63.5hrs)

The Financial Director of Barr Wallace Arnold was one of three sponsors of the Tapestry who increased the amount of requested sponsorship. At a meeting in 1996 Richard Bell was so enthusiastic about the project that Kate was floating on air for a week. "This is it!" she thought, "now the sponsorship will come rolling in!". She held on to this dream, that at some point people would be telephoning us to offer us money, right to the end – it did happen once or twice!

23.
Stylo Tram
Eileen Tram (12hrs)

Their first coach was bought in 1912 and the founder, Robert Barr used it to carry goods during the week and as a charabanc at the weekend. His aim was to get urban dwellers out of the city, first on day trips and by 1921 for whole weeks to Scotland, Devon or the south coast. By 1925 he owned 25 coaches and also had bought the businesses of Wallace Cunningham and Arnold Crowe (35).

34.
X35 Rider Bus
Olwen Poulter (15hrs)

A huge debt of gratitude is also owed to Stuart Baker of Regional Railways NE who spent many hours explaining and drawing maps and diagrams to show the development of railways and the positions of stations. Most people today do not realise there was another station on Wellington Street (Central Station) until the 1950s and that stations sometimes changed locations over 100 years ago!

14.
Royal Mail Van
Godfrey Harland (40hrs)

The 1840 map (1), hand

stitched onto a glazed parchment-coloured cotton by Ann Wheatley, was folded authentically, pressed and stitched into shape. It was then stressed by being left lying around for weeks, stained and eventually baked at medium temperature in the oven. All in an attempt to suitably 'age' and fix the creases. Georgina Day and Kate had spent hours doing tests on various weights of cotton cambrics and linens with coffee, tea and paints, then baking the results. Kate did not know whether to laugh or cry the first time someone said: "What a pity you couldn't get the stains out of the cloth...!"

When stitching the sections to the backcloth Kate was reluctant to stitch the 'maps' too much, as her aim was to keep the folds and the 'lift' that characterises a map just opened out. However during the two and half years since it has been stitched the fabric has moved and sagged to such an extent that it now needs re-stitching. Kate's hand, machine stitched and placed in the bottom corner gives scale to the effect of the maps all being spread out on a large table.

The oldest map represented is by John Cossins from 1726. His note book for making this and his maps of Scarborough and York were auctioned by Sothebys in 1993, bought by the City of York Archivist and

have now been published with notes. The 1840 and 1900s maps illustrate how many roads from all directions converge on the city centre, bringing industrial prosperity. The most recent map shows the loop roads designed to keep traffic away from the city centre to improve the environment for pedestrians. Bicycles are represented by Brian Jackson's delivery bike of the 1940s, a cyclist wearing his safety gear and, finally, a modern cycle path.

Most of the sponsors for this panel were secured before Sylvia joined the Tapestry in 1997, however she brought on board the Classic Car Co. and the Leeds Swordfish Society. Barry Brown of the Society was immensely enthusiastic and amongst other things arranged for Professor Blackburn and his daughter, grandson and great grand-daughter of the aviation pioneer, to attend the unveiling of the panel in January 2000 at the Marriott Hotel. The legendary Swordfish served throughout the Second World War and of the 2,391 built 1,700 were assembled in Yorkshire at the Blackburn Aircraft

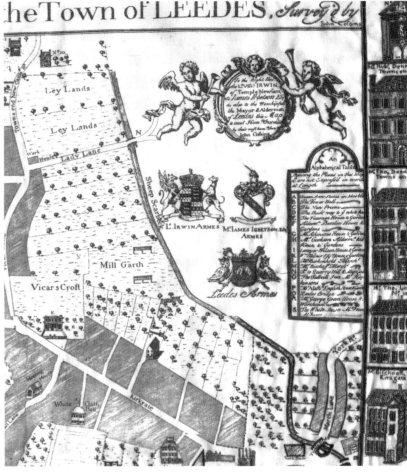

Company's works at Sherburn in Elmet. The oldest surviving example (25), built in 1941, was adopted by Leeds City Council in 1996 and is still flying today, helping to raise funds at many International Airshows. Blackburn's also had a factory on Roundhay Road (the site of Tesco) and many remember how they used to test their new aircraft on Soldier's Field.

The completed unframed panel was exhibited at the Civic Hall during a reunion event of the Leeds Swordfish Appeal. Betty Bertrand and Kate carried the panel from the Civic Hall back to the workspace at Holy Trinity Church to save the cost of hiring a van. There is an embroidery of their moving the *On the Move* panel, produced by Betty, on the *Community Spirit* panel and it is also shown on the front of our small book.

6.
Cossin's Map
Joan Holah (100hrs)

15.
Metro Hotline
Barbara Gray (5hrs)

28.
GNER Coaster
Eileen Wilson

Leeds in Bloom

1. Pink Flower

2. Butterfly
Renee Silverman (2hrs)

3. Primroses
Margaret Foxcroft

4. Butterfly
Audrey Pidgeon (5hrs)

5. Dragonfly
Anna McL Dabbs

6. Butterfly
Audrey Pidgeon (5hrs)

7. Spider's Web
Margaret Foxcroft

8. Butterfly
Valerie Horner (6.5hrs)

9. Grey Ivy
Freda Copley

10. Brown leaves
Joan Holah

11. Leaf

12. Leaf
Merel Jackson

13. Leaf

14. Ivy leaves
Freda Copley

15. Virginia Creeper
Margaret Foxcroft

16. Yellow Flower
Shirley Gale

17. Sunflower
Margaret Foxcroft

18. Sunflower
Margaret Foxcroft

19. Sunflower
Margaret Foxcroft

20. Sunflower

21. Sunflower
Margaret Foxcroft

22. Sunflower
Gill Cook

23. Sunflower
Gill Cook

24. Sunflower
Gill Cook

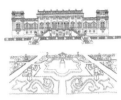

25. Harewood Stables
G Harland & E Wilson

26. Harewood House
The Countess of Harewood
27. Harewood Garden
Betty Bertrand

28. Harewood Estate
Janet Taylor

29. Coronation House
Catherine Davies
30. Roundhay Park Garden
Jack Marlowe

31. Paul Hinds Building
Diane Taylor

32. Gardening Which
Renee Davidson

33. Oulton Hall
E. Malm & M. Kenny

34. The Queen's Hotel
Audrey Gabbitas (437hrs)

35. Oakwood Clock
Maureen Carr & Godfrey
Harland (199hrs)

36. Ainsley's & Mrs Ainsley
Lizzie Ingle, Ann Wheatley
and Jill Rutter (32hrs)

37. Harewood Arms
Harewood Ladies

38. Brethericks
Kath Bretherick & Staff

39. 'My Garden'
Elizabeth Bidgood

40. Temple Newsam
Auriol Moore (400Hrs)

41. Trees in Israel
Muriel Gabbitas

42. Harewood Coat of Arms
The Countess of Harewood &
Betty Bertrand (38hrs)

43. Crowne Plaza Hotel
Godfrey Harland (80hrs)

44. Kirkstall Abbey
Maureen Hinds

45. 9 Woodhouse Square
Muriel Gabbitas

46. Flower Border
Muriel Gabbitas

47. Flower Border
Muriel Gabbitas

48. Nasturtiums
Patricia Andrews

49. Flower Border
Ruth Fowler & Lynne Ward

50. Ford & Warren
Mary Mawson

51. Wedding Car
Karen Pattison (2hrs)

52. Lady with Flowers
Joyce James

53. Owl & Oak
Freda Copley

54. Dog
Valerie Horner (2.5hrs)

55. Joe Maiden
Merel Jackson (11hrs)

56. Bridal Couple
Karen Pattison (2hrs)

57. Leaf

58. Leaf

59. Leaf

60. Leaf

61. Leaf

62. Leaf

63. Oak Leaf

64. Ivy Leaf
Joan Lister

65. Leaf

66. Ivy Leaf

67. Ivy Leaf

68. Oak Leaf

69. Ivy Leaf

70. Ivy Leaf
Merel Jackson

71. Ivy Leaf

72. Ivy Leaf
Freda Copley

72b. Leaf
Freda Copley

73. Leaf

74 Leaf
Joan Holah

75. Leaf

79. Blackberry
Hilary Thurlow

76. Frog
Hilary Thurlow (5hrs)

77. Leaves

78. Nasturtium Leaf

80. Oak Leaf

81. Holly Leaves
Freda Copley

82. Ivy Leaf

83. Winter Leaves
Margaret Foxcroft

84. Winter Leaves
Muriel Gabbitas

85. Clematis
Margaret Foxcroft

86. Winter Ferns
Barbara Walker (2hrs)

87. Autumn Leaves
Muriel Gabbitas

88. Spray of Ivy
Shirley Gale

89. Spray of Ivy
Valerie Horner

90. Spray of Ivy

91. Spray of Ivy
Margaret Foxcroft

92. Spray of Ivy

93. Spray of Ivy
Margaret Foxcroft

94. Spray of Ivy
Valerie Horner

95. Spray of Ivy
Val Gomersall

96. Berries

97. Winter Leaves
Vera Harrington

98. Spray of Ivy
Margaret Foxcroft

99. Spray of Ivy
Shirley Gale

100. Honesty Seeds
Freda Copley

101. Ivy Leaves
Freda Copley

102. Frosted Ivy
Joan Lister

103. Yellow Flowers
Vera Harrington

104. Ivy, Fern, Dandelion
Barbara Walker (10hrs)

105. Butterflies
Sylvia Crowther (6hrs)

106. Leaves
Muriel Gabbitas

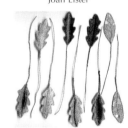

107. Leaves
Pat Smith (48hrs)

108. Leaves

109. Spray of Ivy

110. Ivy Leaves
Shirley Shaw

Detail of Autumn Leaves (87)

111. Ivy Leaf
Freda Copley

112. Machined Leaves

113. Spray of Ivy
Janet Carding

114. Narcissus
Margaret Foxcroft

115. Pink Flower

116. Tulip
Margaret Foxcroft

117. Orchid
Margaret Foxcroft

118. Daffodil
Margaret Foxcroft

119. Pink Flower

120. Daisy

121. Primrose
Margaret Foxcroft

122. Iris
Margaret Foxcroft

123. Cowslip
Margaret Foxcroft

124. Daisies

125. Winter Leaves
Joan Lister

126. Lilac
Hilary Thurlow

127. Leaves & Catkin
Hilary Thurlow

128. Pink Daisy
Mandy Gomersall

129. Daisy

130. Daisies
Shirley Gale

131. Tulip
Margaret Foxcroft

132. Catkins
Freda Copley

133. Snowdrop
Freda Copley

134. Ivy Leaf

135. Ivy Leaf

136. Ivy Leaf

137. Ivy Leaf

138. Ivy Leaf

139. Ivy Leaf
Vera Harrington

140. Leaflets
Vera Harrington

141. Ivy Leaf
Vera Harrington

142. Ivy Leaf
Vera Harrington

143. Ivy Leaf

144. Bryan's Logo
Carol Wurr

145. SGP
Maureen Elvidge

146. Crowne Plaza
Joyce Maynard (5hrs)

147. Gardening Which
M. Glenn (12hrs)
148. Mr and Mrs Ziff Ribbon
Joyce James

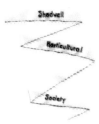

149. Shadwell H.S.
Merel Jackson (4hrs)

150. Oak Leaf

151. Blackberries
Mandy Gomersall

152. Ivy Leaves

153. Butterfly
Audrey Pidgeon (5hrs)

154, Leaves
Hilary Thurlow

155. Leaf

156. Ivy Leaves

157. Daffodils

161. Beetle

158. Nasturtium Leaves
Freda Copley

159. Two Poppies

160. Butterfly
Audrey Pidgeon (5hrs)

162. Ivy Leaf

163. Beetles
Anna McL Dabbs (red)

164. Butterflies

165. Beaded Leaf
Angela Turner

166. Beaded Flower
Angela Turner (15hrs)

167. Oak Leaf

168. Nasturtium Leaf

169. Leaf

170. Leaf

171. Blackberry

44.
Kirkstall Abbey
Maureen Hindes

37.
Harewood Arms
Harewood Ladies
Sewing Circle

34.
The Queen's Hotel
Aubrey Gabbitas
(437hrs)

8.
Butterfly
Valerie Horner (6.5hrs)

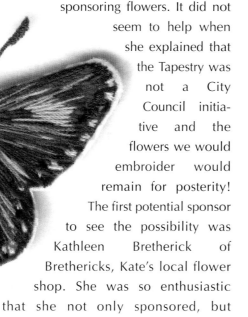

It was always clear to Kate that this panel would be finished but a great number of embroiderers must have had their doubts. When ideas for panel themes were being sought (and even when they were not!) everyone came up with this one. It is obviously a joy to a huge number of people that the City Council do such a fantastic job of planting around the city and the *Leeds in Bloom* competition creates splendid displays all across the city centre.

The Yorkshire Branch of the Embroiderers' Guild expressed their interest in working on the panel very early in the process. In January 1993, after Kate's talk, over 40 members volunteered their skills. Sadly they had to wait a very long time. As always the design would follow the consultation with sponsors. No sponsors – no design.

Kate began by telephoning the hundreds of companies who had won *Leeds in Bloom* prizes or sponsored flower beds. The majority felt they should have a free place on the panel, as they had already supported the city by buying or sponsoring flowers. It did not seem to help when she explained that the Tapestry was not a City Council initiative and the flowers we would embroider would remain for posterity! The first potential sponsor to see the possibility was Kathleen Bretherick of Brethericks, Kate's local flower shop. She was so enthusiastic that she not only sponsored, but

embroidered her piece, enlisting her staff to each sew a brick.

Ainsley's Bakery and Paul Hinds Solicitors also came to the Tapestry via personal contact. They were introduced by Philippa Randall, then Headmistress of Leeds Girls' High School, who had been so supportive with *Education*. Their shared building has been a Leeds in Bloom winner.

It had already been decided to put the Queen's Hotel in place of honour together with City Square. Thinking it may help to bring more sponsors in if they could see a design, Kate set about creating a structure flexible enough to allow future participants to express their creativity. The resulting sketch pictured Kirkstall Abbey in the spring, the Queen's in the summer, the

Tropical House and Rose Garden in the autumn and Harewood in the winter. The side sections were largely blank awaiting future response. The borders between all the sections were designed to show leaves and flowers, both wild and cultivated, from all seasons. Many keen volunteers were eager to get started on the flower borders which were visualised in layers of counted thread work overlaid with three dimensional flowers and leaves. Freda

Copley, an enthusiastic embroiderer and gardener, spent hours collecting cuttings from magazines to create a collage of authentic seasonal borders. Kate used Freda's encyclopaedic books to develop drawings from which Hazel Rand could design the charts ready for the stitchers.

After the first piece of full colour publicity had been in the Yorkshire Evening Post, thirty six cross-stitchers called volunteering to stitch pieces. The panel was designed mainly in counted thread work as a response to this demand.

Somewhat dismayed by the lack of progress on the sponsorship front and feeling she needed help, Kate approached the Council's Leeds in Bloom Committee to ask if she could give them a brief presentation about the project. She took designs and beautiful samples of finished flowers and leaves, as well as photographs of completed panels to show to them at the end of their meeting, hoping to engage them in suggesting ideas and helping with publicity. Unfortunately they were not at all interested. Just one member said he would like to have his cafe pictured on the panel. Kate followed this through taking photographs and making sketches, introducing hanging baskets and outside tables to brighten up the rather seedy frontage. When the piece was almost finished, including one of Audrey Pidgeon's lace tablecloths to enhance the al fresco dining, Kate found the proprietor had vanished without trace. This was the last time a sponsored piece was made without first receiving the cheque, even though at times this slowed down the process considerably.

Fortunately at about this time Barbara Cresswell, former fund-raiser at Wheatfields Hospice, joined the Tapestry team for a few short years. She brought a fresh approach and new energy for completing this panel,

Detail of Autumn Leaves
Muriel Gabbitas

39.
'My Garden'
Elizabeth Bidgood

129.
Daisy

26.
Harewood House
The Countess of
Harewood
27.
Harewood Garden
Betty Bertrand

40.
Temple Newsam
Auriol Moore (400hrs)

as well as freeing more of Kate's time for designing and the trusts she enlisted were willing to support the panel without reprsentation on it. However Barbara experienced similar difficulties in getting companies on board - so many were enthusiastic until it came to writing a cheque!

And so another lull until Sylvia brought her contacts from *Gardening Which*, a generous contribution from Mrs Audrey Burton and, much later in the project, in-kind sponsorship from The Crowne Plaza and Oulton De Vere Hotels. *Gardening Which* supplied wonderful photographs of sunflowers and Joe Maiden working at Golden Acre Park.

Meanwhile Kath Bretherick had been talking to everyone she knew about the panel. She was as frustrated as we were at the slow progress and introduced the Harewood Arms with a group of Harewood embroiderers willing to stitch its frontage for the panel.

Members of this group told Kate that the Countess of Harewood was an experienced needlewoman. This was exciting news! Harewood House had already been suggested by Audrey Gabbitas as the main piece for the winter section. Kate wondered if she could ask the Countess if she would like to embroider her own House and Garden, knowing that her involvement would greatly help to raise the profile of the whole Tapestry and therefore of textile art itself.

Lady Harewood not only agreed to stitch the house, which was elegantly charted by

19.
Sunflower
Margaret Foxcroft

Ann Wheatley, but she also played a leading role in the consultation, design and funding which led to the whole of the winter section being Harewood House and Estate. This was just the beginning of a very fruitful and creative relationship with the Countess of Harewood.

Two of the side sections were sponsored by one of the volunteers. Elizabeth Bidgood raised the funds for her own garden and that of Temple Newsam to be embroidered. The former by herself and the latter by her friend Auriol Moore. Kate had wanted to represent a domestic garden on the panel and Elizabeth's was a fine example, not only in reality but also in her interpretation.

The panel can not be discussed without mentioning the leaves. At one time or another all of the volunteers seemed to have made some. Hilary Thurlow's needleweaving workshops were a great success and the method of tacking wire onto a shape drawn onto cardboard with needleweaving across the wire was passed on to many who did not attend the workshops. Many branched out from their usual style of embroidery to have a go. Other leaves were created by hand or machine stitching onto fabric and then cutting round the shape or, in the case of the crystal organza ferns, the stitched outline was burned away from the background fabric using a fine pointed soldering iron and yet others were made in beadwork .

Several attempts had been made over the years by Sylvia and others to remind the Leeds in Bloom Initiative

that the panel was in the final stages and offer the opportunity to have their logo, from which the panel got its name, somewhere amongst the flowers. There had been interest from some members but no firm decision. When Kathleen Bretherick, still waving the flag, became a member of the committee she felt she might be able to raise interest.Disappointingly the committee decided against it and the panel was completed without its title.

There were enormous problems putting the finished sections together. So many people wanted to work in counted thread and the technique is so time consuming that each piece had to be worked on a different piece of canvas or aida. When all of the projects were ready to be joined extra backing had to be put on to compensate for the range of weights of fabric used. Even this failed to stop the sagging, stretching and twisting of the panel as more pieces were added. Much of it had to be unpicked and re-stretched by the famous double act of Shirl and Merel

It was a sheer joy arranging the three dimensional flowers and leaves, marvelling over the botanical perfection of one and the vivid colour of another. Not surprisingly this panel is a great favourite.

Frog
Hilary Thurlow

52.
Lady with Flowers
Joyce James

Faith in the City

1. St Paul's Ireland Wood
Mary Mawson (70hrs)

2. Otley Cross (45hrs)
O. Hudson & G Wolliscroft

3. Owl
Val Gomersall (6hrs)

4. Puritan Church
Eileen Cummings (30hrs)

5. St John's Church
Gill Cook

6. Holy Trinity & Mill Hill
Myra Turner (16hrs)

7. St Anne's Cathedral
Lizzie Ingle & Lynne Ward (50hrs)

8. St George's Church
Joyce James

9. Leeds Parish Church
Joyce James

10. Leeds Parish Church
Godfrey Harland (479hrs)

11. Oxford Place
June Hardy

12. Sikh Temple
Janet Carding (20hrs)

13. Bramhope Church
Mary Mawson

14. Adel Church
Mary Mawson (60hrs)

15. Mill Hill Chapel
M. Cordell & the Congregation

16. St John's Church
Patricia Andrews (260hrs)

17. Oxford Place
Evi Malm (200hrs)

18. Kirkstall Abbey
Edith Vertigan (2176hrs)

19. Synagogue
Pauline Clayden (19.5hrs)

20. St Anne's Cathedral
Barbara Gray (356hrs)

21. Adel Church
Jenny McLean (30hrs)

22. Harehiill's Mosque
Margaret Clark

23. Trees
Margaret Kenny

24. Trees
Margaret Kenny

25. Pagans
Janet Taylor

26. Palm Sunday Procession
Val Gomersall (32hrs)

27. Methodist Meeting
Dorothy Wrench (12hrs)

28. Mosque
Ayesha Dost & Team

29. Medina Mosque
Zuber Mohammed & Team

30. Crowd
Jackie Ford

31. Crowd
Jackie Ford

32. Crowd
Jackie Ford

33. Crowd
Gill Cook

34. Crowd
Gill Cook

35. Wedding Guests
Anne Boyle (24hrs)

36. Crowd
Jackie Ford

37. Family Group
Jackie Ford

38. Rabbi and Boy
Jackie Ford

39. Bridesmaids
Janet Taylor (12hrs)

40. Renee's Family
Renee Silverman

41. Choir Girls
Jackie Ford

42. The Mayor & Bishop Konstant
Claire Wildman (45hrs)

43. Two Men
Jackie Ford

44. Buffalo Methodists
Janet Taylor (7hrs)

45. Trees
Margaret Kenny

46. Choir Boys
Jackie Ford

47. Trees
Margaret Kenny

48. Trees & Bushes
Margaret Kenny

Detail of 37

Detail of 34

49. Louise & Sarah Shaw
Claire Wildman

50. Paul Shaw
Claire Wildman

51. Dr Bernadette Samaranayake
Dorothy Wrench (5hrs)

52. Lady in Sari
Judith Jackson (6hrs)

53. Lady in Salwar-Kameez
Joan Bogunovic

54. Armley Mills Staff
Jackie Ford

55. Sylvia's Mum
Claire Wildman (24hrs)

56. Dr Joseph Samaranayake
Val Gomersall (5hrs)

57. Flagholder
Arshima Team & Ayesha Dost

58. Flagholder
Arshima Team & Ayesha Dost

59. Claire Shaw
Audrey Pidgeon

60. Lady in Red
Maureen Carr

61. Man from St George's
Jackie Ford

62. Man
Jackie Ford

63. First Communion Girl
June Adams & Friends

Concord Ladies

64. Concord Ladies
Anne Wragg

65. Asian Lady

66. Man with blue turban

67. Man from St George's
Jackie Ford

68. Back view of Lady
Ann Barker

69.

70. Nicolas
Audrey Gabbitas (41hrs)

71. Boy with candle
Ayesha Dost

72. Girl with Candle
Janet Taylor

73. Eileen Cummings
Eileen Cummings

74. Brian Jackson
Merel Jackson (6.5hrs)

75. Peter Crowther
Janet Taylor (3hrs)

76. Pat Potton
Merel Jackson (10hrs)

77. Monseigneur MaGuire
Claire Wildman (20hrs)

78. Anthony Norcliffe
Sheila Exley (2hrs)

79. Mr & Mrs Gamble
Joan Gamble & Janet Taylor

80. Cllr Peggy White

81. Man
Jackie Ford

82. Man with Blue Shirt

83. Man
Sikh Ladies Group

84. Harvey Goodman
Renee Silverman

85. Harvey Silverman
Renee Silverman

86. Man
Jackie Ford

87. Boy
Jackie Ford

88. Asian Dancer
Zuber Mohammed Team

89. Brownies (Ireland Wood)
Mary Mawson

94. Two Ladies

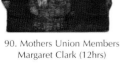

90. Mothers Union Members
Margaret Clark (12hrs)

91. First Communion Boys
Janet Taylor

92. Man
Val Horner

93. Three Boys

95. Sky
Mary Mawson & Janet Taylor

96. Gargoyle

97. Celtic Cross
Karen Pattison (4hrs)

98. John Harrison
Janet Taylor (6hrs)

99. Menorah
Jackie Ford

100. Peace Doves
Anne Wragg

101. Diocese of Leeds
Cath Stewart (12hrs)

102. Churches Together
Pauline Dean (4hrs)

103. Star of David
Barbara Gray

104. Moravian Flag
M. Milne & E. Wilson

105. United Reformed Church
Janet Carding

106. Buddhist Wheel
Freda Hooper (9hrs)

107. Alwoodley Park
Judith Jackson (4.5hrs)

108. Roundhay & Thorner
Barbara Farrugia (6hrs)

109. Binn's Organ
Anne Boyle (80hrs)

110. Green Man
Jackie Wilkinson (100hrs)

111. The Lord's Prayer
Eileen Cummings (10hrs)

115. Christian Aid Cross
Claire Wildman

112. Quakers
Margaret Booth

113. Gloria in Excelsis
Eileen Wilson

114. Candle

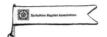

116.The Grove Methodists

117. Yorkshire Baptists
Merel Jackson (6hrs)

118. Wesley Rd. Chapel
Claire Wildman (4hrs)

119. Leeds Methodist Choir
Judith Jackson
120. Christian Aid
Audrey Pidgeon (15hrs)

121. Sanctuary for All
Eileen Cummings (14hrs)

122. Save the Children
M Glenn (10hrs)
123. Hospices Flag
Betty Hoggart

124. Concord
Anne Wragg

125. St George's Crypt
Eileen Cummings (2hrs)
126. Fox
Mary Mawson

127. Cafod
Mrs A Bellwood (10hrs)

131. Circle of Goddesses
Joan Holah (26hrs)

128. Trade for Change
Claire Wildman (30.5hrs)

129. Christian Science
Marie Whaley

LEEDS JEWISH COMMUNITY
& LUBAVITCH WISH YOU A
HAPPY CHANUKAH

130. Chanukah
Eileen Cummings (4hrs)

132. Methodist Homes
Joan Holah (4hrs)

133. Traidcraft
Janet Carding

134. South Parade Baptists
Cynthia Shipley (20hrs)

135. Bahai Faith Group
Liz Firth (3.5hrs)

136. Tibetan Buddhist Flag

137. One Faith
J. Carding & S Exley

138. Holy Trinity Church

139. Sikh Symbol
Joyce James (5hrs)

140. Salvation Army
Joan Holah

141. Buddhist Wheel
Mrs A Bellwood (8hrs)

142. URC
Cynthia Shipley (4hrs)

143. Mother's Union
Joan Holah (4.5hrs)

144. Hindu Symbol
Joan Holah

145. Bahai Symbol
Joan Holah

146. Symbol of Islam
Joyce James (5hrs)

Faith in the City
DIVERSE CONGREGATIONS

136.
Tibetan Buddhist Flag

19.
Synagogue
Pauline Clayden
(19.5hrs)

14.
Adel Church
Mary Mawson (60hrs)

72.
Girl with candle
Janet Taylor

29.
Medina Mosque
Zuber Mohammed
& Team

The first formal consultation took place at Armley Mills Museum in 1996. Kate was overjoyed; there were so many different faiths groups represented under one roof! Many people informally consulted earlier had expressed their doubt that an Interfaith panel was a possibility.

There was a great deal of energy and goodwill in the group which included Concord Interfaith Group and COLECT as well as representatives from Quakers and Baptists. Many of its members worked on the project in some way; either embroidering sections, writing pieces for magazines, encouraging sponsorship or attending Tapestry workshops and events. Sylvia Crowther who was representing the Methodist Church became the greatest funding resource for the project when in 1997 she became Fundraiser. This group also provided many ideas and photographs of choirs, weddings, churches and individuals. Even with all this effort and goodwill, the names and contacts from the Hindu, Jewish, Muslin, and Sikh communities failed to bear fruit. Kate spent more time and energy attempting to encourage their participation than on the whole of the rest of the panel. The three successes were all towards the end of the project and all of them personal contacts.

Ayesha Dost contacted us and was confident that she could raise money in the Muslim community to have a mosque represented. She tried over many years but in the end made a small donation personally and contributed many pieces of embroidery to *Faith in the City* and *Community Spirit*.

After a series of pleasant but largely unfruitful conversations with various individuals and organisations within the Jewish community (including some from passionate and vocal volunteers) we had a stroke of luck. During the 1999 exhibition at Harewood House we were introduced to Arnold and Marjorie Ziff who saved the day by sponsoring the 'New Synagogue' (now the home of the Northern School of Contemporary Dance). Recreating the synagogue including the stained glass window and the Hebrew text was greatly helped by the kindness and generosity of Rabbis Ian D Morris and Solomon Brown and by Eve Charing. The Tapestry Project commissioned photographer Paul Wilkinson to record the Menorah lighting ceremony outside the Town Hall in 2001 and Renee Silverman provided the personal touch with the photographs and delightful embroideries of her family. This, of course, is what Kate wanted for every faith - to be able to show highlights from all religious calendars and events from

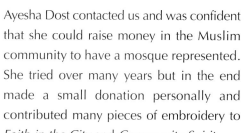

39.
Bridesmaids
Janet Taylor (12hrs)

all faiths so that *Faith in the City* could extend understanding and religious tolerance or, at least, provide some insight to each faith.

The greatest insight she got was an understanding of why there are still religious wars raging in the world. We had a few in the studio and workroom where individuals from various groups were insisting that the symbol of their faith could not be touching, next to or even on the same panel as the symbols of other faiths. What hope is there for peace and harmony in the world if even to create visual harmony is such a problem?

The first actual sponsor for the panel was Joan Gamble, on behalf of Mill Hill Chapel. Joan is one of the stalwart enthusiasts who has seen the whole project from the exciting beginning, through all the downs and ups to its successful conclusion. She not only

organised events to raise funds for and awareness of the Tapestry but she also sponsored some pieces, embroidered others and attended many workshops and events. She and her late husband, treasurer of the Chapel for over 40 years, are depicted on the panel in their wedding outfits.

The Leeds Church Institute generously provided sufficient funds to support the representation of the City Churches and the symbols (provided by Concord) of other faiths. Kate spent a great deal of time running workshops and giving slide talks at temples and mosques – all with the support of Garry Barker at the Leeds College of Art. The project commissioned photographs of events from Jan Wells and others who had friends in Sikh and Hindu communities. Kate also photographed women at the workshops and helped several of them to paint or embroider their own images so that people from both faiths are represented on the panel. Interpreters were hired so that the civic nature of the project could be properly explained, but still Kate was unable to inspire full participation.

Towards the end of 2001 the Trustees of the Tapestry supported the proposal that we subsidise the inclusion of a representation of the Harehills Mosque and the Sikh

Opposite
Kirkstall Abbey
Enid Gator-not used

79.
Mr & Mrs Gamble
Joan Gamble
& Janet Taylor

88. Opposite
Asian Dancer
Zuber Mohammed
& Team

12.
Sikh Temple
Janet Carding (20hrs)

One of the original paintings for the churches by James Brown.

4.
Puritan Church
Eileen Cummings (30hrs)

13. Opposite
Bramhope Church
Mary Mawson

1.
St.Paul's Ireland Wood
Mary Mawson (70hrs)

98.
John Harrison
Janet Taylor (6hrs)

18.
Kirkstall Abbey
Edith Vertigan (2176hrs)

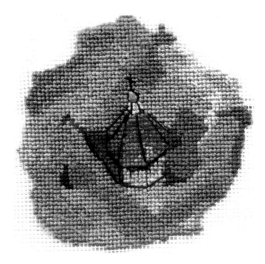

Temple in Chapeltown (both photographed by Paul). Photocopies of these images were then sent to representatives of both faith groups to ensure there was no objection.

Churches, chapels and many groups and congregations seemed to present themselves fairly effortlessly, though several people were active behind the scenes to ensure this happened. Sylvia,

Sister Bernadette, Monsignor McGuire, Reverends David Rhodes and Nick Howe and Margaret Morrish were all instrumental in encouraging church groups and organisations into the Tapestry fold. Volunteers Mary Mawson, Claire Wildeman, Cynthia Shipley and Judith Jackson all encouraged or provided funds for their church or chapel to be embroidered. Mary held church events, baking and making craft items to raise the funds. She also provided photographs or drawings of St Paul's, Ireland Wood and Adel and Bramhope Churches.

John Harrison (1579-1656), originally intended for *Local Faces*, appears beside St John's Church which he paid to have built. He was a cloth merchant who bought properties and used the rents to finance acts of charity. The charitable trusts he set up before his death still benefit the people of Leeds.

The design process also had a rather tortuous start. Having seen the 'three-dimensional' picture maps by James Brown, Kate wondered if

77.
Monsignor McGuire
Claire Wildman (20hrs)

36.
Crowd
Jackie Ford

he might be persuaded to draw the churches (and temples, mosques, etc as they 'arrived') from an aerial perspective like the city maps. She thought that this device might lend visual unity to the work. He was delighted to do so and did a wonderful job. In fact, the watercolours were so delicate that it is difficult to do justice to them in the embroidery.

The church leaders and congregations preferred their buildings seen from street level and so in many cases both have been used in juxtaposition. From then on the design process was pretty smooth. There were the usual hiccups of course, when projects got stuck somewhere in the production line or came out an unexpected colour, shape or size. Towards the end, when the pieces were being stitched to the panel, Kate realised more congregations and trees were needed at the top. Gill Cooke, Jackie Ford and Margaret Kenny obliged, producing amazing results at very short notice. Margaret Booth embroidered the Quaker piece (112) based on the unique and enchanting Quaker Tapestry in Kendal.

The collation process, which Kate thought might be tricky was in fact very enjoyable. The whole thing came together really well with the help of many volunteers working hundreds of hours stitching down the many square feet of 'buildings'.

The sky, largely hand-stitched in a mammoth attempt by Mary Mawson, had to be somehow visually linked to the machine embroidery done by Janet Taylor. Even this was enjoyable, layering nets and introducing a misty moon. The final touch for Kate was a joyful day spent with her daughter Victoria, painting shadows, linking the larger 'greensward' with the rich grassy grounds of Kirkstall Abbey and critiquing and appraising the ever growing number of completed panels.

106.
Buddhist Wheel
Freda Hooper (9hrs)

63.
First Commubion Girl
June Adams & Friends

112.
Quakers
Margaret Booth

9.
Leeds Parish Church
Joyce James

1. Old Museum, Park Row
Godfrey Harland (73hrs)

2. Tudor Girl
Joan Holah(90hrs)

3. Henry Moore Sculpture
Ruth Seaman & B Bertrand

4. Paula Rego Poster
Joan Holah(70hrs)

5. Roman Mosaic
Karen Pattison (27hrs)

6. Egyptian Mummy
Betty Laycock

7. Armley Mills
Chris Richardson

8. Lotherton Hall
Anne Cove

9. . Elephant
Mrs M Dawes (40hrs)

10. Landscape
Kay Royce

11. Landscape
Mildred Keedy

12. Patchwork Sample

13. Andy Goldsworthy
Janet Taylor

14. Mary Lord Painting
Merel Jackson (14hrs)

15. Bluebell Wood
Ann Cove

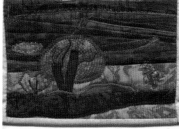

16. Stone Walls, Malham
Liz Thompson

17. Pillars at Catalana
Chris Richardson

In 1993 the Yorkshire Branch of the Embroiderers' Guild wanted to take on the whole of the *Leeds in Bloom* panel. Kate was inspired by this enthusiastic response, and began to include this idea in subsequent talks she gave to other textile groups. So it was that, in 1995, the Night Owls quilting group, under the leadership of Chris Richardson, expressed an interest in constructing one of the Art panels.

There were frustrating delays in getting started, with the usual problem of raising sponsorship. Several of the proposed panels such as those on history, nature, geography, community, food and fashion failed to get off the ground for this reason, with no interest being expressed. Conversations to generate ideas still went on with whoever was willing to talk about them. Jude Kelly, Artistic Director at the West Yorkshire Playhouse; Peter Brears, author and historian; Gail Bolland at Tonic; Dr Kevin Grady and Dr Evelyn Silber, then Director of Museums and Galleries, were all approached. Discussions were also held with staff and visitors at the various museums and galleries, artists and volunteers' friends. These discussions centred around what should be the content of an Arts Panel. Should it be visual and/or performing arts? What painting, sculpture, piece of music or dance that you have seen in Leeds inspires you?

Gradually the idea formed of creating the image of a decorative pin-board that might be in the office of the Director of Museums and Galleries. On it would be a collection of posters, prints, postcards, photographs showing a range of art objects and activities; perhaps a letter or card from an artist, composer or dancer; with the challenge of recreating all this in embroidery.

Armley Mills
Machine appliqued
by Chris Richardson

3.
Henry Moore
Sculpture
Ruth Seaman

18.
Bluebell Wood
Anne Cove

14.
Mary Lord Painting
Merel Jackson (14hrs)

10.
Landscape
Kay Royce

17.
Pillars at Catalana
Chris Richardson

By this time, around 1997/98, when Kate was designing this decorative 'pinboard' in a way that she hoped would be enjoyable for the Night Owls to piece together, many of the group were busy doing other things. However Chris and three others made the most beautiful sample 'postcards' to see what could be done on that scale and also to help inspire sponsorship and further participation.

At this point Kate went back to the group with new slides for the completed panels and with the proposed design for the 'pinboard' to try and revive interest in the flagging project. There was still zero funding and not even a conversation with a possible sponsor, so it was difficult to finalise a design for what would be pinned to the decorative backcloth. Kate decided to work on a few pieces which had been suggested by many people and hoped this would encourage funding.

Chris fortunately was still very enthusiastic and set about making the pieced work

almost single-handedly. She also applied, successfully, for a small grant for material expenses to the Leeds Voluntary and Community Sector Initiative (1999). The team could not believe it - the first funding for the Arts panel in over five years of trying - would this be a turning point?

By the time Chris had completed the quilt, contact had been made with the Leeds Art Collection Fund through Barbara Roberts (a trustee) who was very keen to have one of their new acquisitions featured on the panel. Paula Rego's work was the selection and was duly embroidered by Joan Holah. This remained the only sponsored piece for the panel by the beginning of 2002 and it was increasingly obvious that it would not be ready for the exhibition of the other fifteen panels. Then Sylvia Crowther and Barclays Bank created a miracle!

Sylvia had applied for awards from many sources to enable us to put on an

closed and after this book was finished, to complete the Arts panel bit by bit. The intention was to work, as in the beginning, with Kate's home and studio as the base. Now the volunteers have the extraordinary luxury of being able to work on the *Arts for All* panel not only without the pressure of having to raise funds but with complete freedom of design.

Thank you Barclays!

Thank you Sylvia for helping us to end on a high note!

Janet Taylor's machine embroidery based on one of Andy Goldsworthy's pieces.

2.
Tudor Girl
Joan Holah (90hrs)

exhibition worthy of the project and the stately venue at Harewood House. More in desperation than in hope a number of potential donors had been approached for assistance with the languishing *Arts for All* panel. Barclays came up trumps with a generous grant, split equally between funding for the printing and other exhibition costs and the production of *Arts for All*. They also showed enthusiasm for the project by sending staff to various practical workshops and other events, including the private view at Harewood.

Since the exhibition had been designed nine months earlier, in consultation with staff at Harewood House, and the catalogue, brochure and banners were already with the printer, it was too late to include even the part-worked *Arts for All* panel in the show. It had always been the intention after the exhibition, after the office and production space had been cleared and

11.
Landscape
Mildred Keedy

5.
Roman Mosaic
Karen Pattison (27hrs)

Elephant at the Armouries appliqued by Mrs M Dawes.

LS 2000

1. Asda Building
Barbara Hebden

2. B & N Housing
Janet Taylor (7.5hrs)

3. Bartlett Building
Lesley Dove (31hrs)

4. Privilege Building
Joan Holah (30hrs)

5. Rushbond Building
Betty Bertrand

6. Brewster Bye Building
Joan Holah (20hrs)

7. Teesland Building
Jan Brown (200hrs)

8. Rushbond Building
Myra Turner

9. Kirkgate Market
Joan Holah (89hrs)

10. Abbey Holford Rowe
Janet Taylor

11. Drawn Metal Gates
Renee Silverman

12. National Westminster Bank
Evi Malm (160hrs)

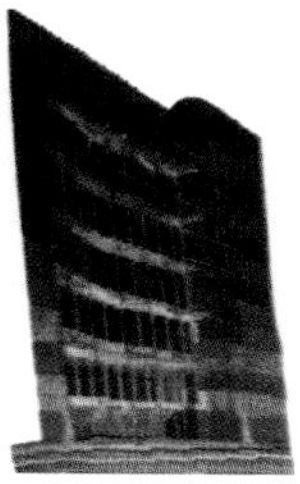

13. Carey Jones Building
Jan Brown

14. Springfield House
Joan Holah (200hrs)

15. Tetley Brewery
Betty Bertrand (40hrs)

16. Pool Court
Hanni Gill (60hrs)

17. Birse
Joyce James

18. British Waterways
Liz Firth (8hrs)

19. Tetley Brewery
Mary Mawson (128hrs)

20. Marriott Hotel
Joan Holah

21. White Rose Centre
R. Silverman & M Kenny

22. White Rose Centre
Janet Carding (33hrs)

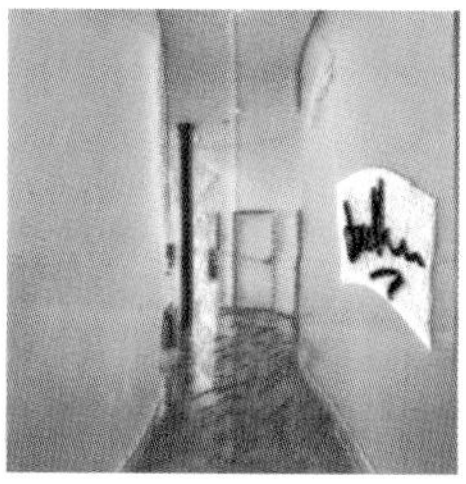

23. Jonathan Morgan's
Joan Holah (8hrs)

24. Sample
Maggie Grey

25. Arup
Joyce Maynard

26. Price Waterhouse Cooper
Denise Teed

27. Royal Armouries
Maureen Elvidge

28. DTZ
Joyce Maynard
29. Teesland Flag
Jackie Moore (4hrs)

30. Owl
Joyce James (30hrs)

31. GWP
Joyce Maynard

32. Abbey Holford Rowe
Eileen Cummings (1hr)

33. Henderson Insurance
Mavis Glenn
34. Bell Cablemedia
Mavis Glenn (3hrs)

35. Drawn Metal Ltd
Renee Silverman

36. Marriott Logo
Joyce Maynard (5hrs)
37. GWP
Eileen Cummings (1hr)

38. Thistle Hotels
Ann Boyle (15hrs)

39. B & N Housing
Eileen Cummings (1hr)

40. Carey Jones
Joyce Maynard

41. LS 2000 Logo
Janet Taylor

42. LS 2000 Logo
Zuber Mohammed Team

43. The Light and DLG
Joyce Maynard

44. Privilege Insurance

45. Redmayne Bentley
Eileen Wilson (6hrs)

46. Websites
E Cummings & M Clark

47. GVA Grimley
Jan Brown (12hrs)
48. Walker Morris Solicitors
Gwen Woolliscroft (8hrs)

49. Lamp
50. The Black Prince
Elizabeth Thackrah

51. River
Elizabeth Thackrah

52. Plan of Corn Exchange
Elizabeth Thackrah

53. Civic Hall Owl
Beryl Smith

54. Black Prince
Maggie Grey

55. Bartlett
Judith Reynolds (12hrs)

56. CDW
Janet Carding

57. Coutts Bank
Jan Brown

58. BT Logo
Barbara Walker (2hrs)

59. Dacre Son & Hartley
June Stockwell

The Tapestry Team almost lost track of how many names this panel had been given and how many different ideas and themes were eventually metamorphosed into *LS2000*.

As always the changes were made in response to the growing (or shrinking!) body of sponsors. After the unveiling of the *Money Works* panel there were other banks, stockbrokers and insurers who had not been included for one reason or another. They were now calling for a second financial services panel. The talk was of 24-hour and Internet Banking and the new call centres so we hoped to create a panel about the world wide web and a whole new framework for global money transactions.

During the last 10 years or so of the second Millennium the built environment of Leeds changed dramatically.

Much new development was springing up all around the city, especially around the waterfront, including cafes, bars and leisure complexes. The title *Urban Fabric* emerged. This would represent the extraordinary regeneration of Leeds City centre perhaps focussed on the waterfront.

Kate waited to see which of these potential panels (*Communications, Urban Fabric* or *Financial Services II*) would be sponsored first. Meanwhile work continued on the idea of including fibre optics within the embroidery. This was first suggested in 1996 by Nicki Embleton of Bell Cable Media (now ntl).

Between 1997 and 1999 Kate investigated fibre optics. She attended workshops, talked to engineers, bought cheap fibre optics lamps and Christmas lights (and took them apart!) as well as talking to experts at colleges and

7.
Teesland Building
Jan Brown (200hrs)

universities. Finally, having been provided with funding by British Telecom to do the research, Kate was able to enter into the process more fully. She attended a workshop organised by Chrysalis Arts on the use of fibre optics by Artists. The workshop was exciting, the idea looked possible. She saw slides and demonstrations of all kinds of uses: exterior, interior, huge cables and thread-like fibres, all carrying this beautiful low-energy no-maintenance light.

Late in 1999, Fibre Optics FX gave a demonstration workshop for the volunteers and lent them all the equipment they needed to experiment themselves. The volunteers

devised all manner of ways of stitching, threading, overlocking and twisting the fibres into the Internet 'Super Highway'. The proposals were costed and only then was it realised that more funds would have to be raised to carry it through.

During this latest stalemate, one of the volunteers brought in a newspaper

article about a fire caused by a fibre optics display. The insurers were informed and it transpired that if fibre optics were to be used in any of the panels, even if all the fabric were fireproofed, they would be uninsurable.

An aesthetic problem also arose. Using fibres as fine as the ones needed, it was discovered that effectively they would only be seen in the dark and so all the wonderfully detailed embroidery would not be seen in daylight. Kate had to consider the extra problems generated by providing a light source for both the fibre optics and the exterior lighting for different panels. This would create unworkable technical demands on future exhibitors of the Tapestry.

30.
Owl
Joyce James (30hrs)

2.
B&N Group
Janet Taylor (7.5hrs)

1.
Asda Building
Barbara Hebden

stalls both in Leeds and abroad for beads, sequins and anything that glittered. Eventually Elizabeth Thrackrah (Tapestry road and river specialist) put the Internet 'Super Highway' together with dark blue vilene, a gift from Freudenbergs, together with layers of net, wires and holographic foil.

Meanwhile, back in the office, the new sponsors coming on board were largely architects and developers. This was partly due to Kate's attendance, with her husband, at a series of architecture seminars held at the LMU and organised by Allen Todd

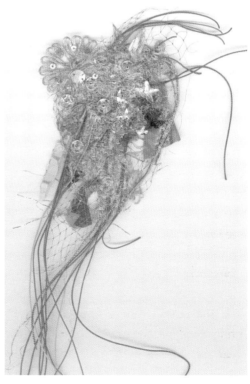

22.
White Rose Centre
Janet Carding (33hrs)

18. Above right
British Waterways
Liz Firth (8hrs)

Sample from Diane Bates Workshop.

At this point Kate reluctantly decided to abandon the use of fibre optics.

Back again to the drawing board! Yet more experimental workshops were held, using computer aided design, machine embroidery and Orise fabric with Maggie and Clive Grey (see the windows in the Evans 'sample' No.24). A mixed media workshop with Diane Bates included all the workings of a mother board. Volunteers scoured the market

Architects, but mostly due to Sylvia's persistence in following them up!

During the year 2000 it became clear that the panel themes *Communications, Urban Fabric,* and *Financial Services II* would be amalgamated into one panel. This was mainly because there was no way another underfunded panel could be subsidised but also because all the themes seemed to fit well around the central drawing.

Darren Newby of Carey Jones had already been commissioned to design an architectural map for *Urban Fabric,* including the City Square statues. Kate thought the juxtaposition of the river, the 'super highway frame' and the map embroidered on vilene, with the embroidered buildings raised on polyboard, worked well – thanks to Darren for the inspiration! As a thriving architectural practice, founded only in 1987, Carey Jones represent the new Leeds with their building in Park Row interpreted on the panel by Jan Brown. Other new buildings on *LS 2000* include those sponsored by Brewster Bye, Privilege Insurance, Teesland, the Goddard Wybor Practice, Rushbond, the B & N Group and National Westminster Bank.

The *LS2000* logo which features twice on this panel and once in 'lights' (actually in beads!) on *Community Spirit* is used with the permission of the Millennium Office of the Leeds City Council to show appreciation for a grant from the Leeds City Council Community Chest.

The title *LS2000* suggesting a postcode brings together geographical location, the year and co-incidentally the approximate

11.
Drawn Metal Gates
Renee Silverman

13.
Carey Jones Building
Jan Brown

number of people involved in some way in making the whole Tapestry

Putting this panel together was a nightmare for Kate and the Team. The process involved extensively researching specialist conservation glues, several 16-hour days, sleepless nights, hair dryers, lots of breath holding, finger crossing, very heavy books and dozens of boxes of tapestry postcards. The ecstasy you see in the photograph is very largely coloured by relief as it was just finished the hour before Martin Banks came to photograph it for the first book.

What a relief!

17.
Birse
Joyce James

1. The Sun
Mary Mawson (25hrs)

2. The Moon
Betty Bertrand (5hrs)

3. Valentine Fair
Sue Hodgson

4. Arcade Roof (987hrs)
E. Vertigan & Glynis Evans

5. Norwich Union
Hilary Thurlow

6. Leeds Market
Glynis Evans

7. Two Old Ladies
Freda Copley (5hrs)

8. Three Shoppers
TAG

9. Barbara Creswell
Jackie Ford

10. Lady with Pushchair
Jackie Ford

11. Man in Suit
Anna McL Dabbs

12. Backview of Shopper
A. Dabbs or Mary Fletcher

13. Lady in Red
Barbara Blacoe

14. Three Youths
Jackie Ford & Gina Day

15. Table with Menu

16. Couple at Table
Barbara Gray

17. Table & Chairs
Denise Teed

18. Cllr John Trickett
Sheila Udakis

19. Table with Teapot

20. Man on Stilts
Sarah Hodgson

21. Mosaic
Sarah Hodgson

22. Two Ladies Eating
Freda Copley (500hrs)

23. Potted Fern
Freda Copley

24. Lilies
Freda Copley

25. Metro Bag
Barbara Town

26. Burton's Bag
Mary Mawson

27. Debenham's Bag
Merel Jackson

28. Principles Bag
Mary Mawson

29. Harvey Nichols Bag
Vivienne Brown

30. Bass Sign
Vivienne Scott or A Wheatley

31. Samaritan's Phone
Merel Jackson

32. Norwich Union

33. Norwich Union

34. Blue Plaque
Gina Day

35. Flower Baskets
Sue Geldeard

36. Town Hall
Sue Hodgson

37. Hotel Metropole
Clare Bryan

38. Flower Basket
Sue Geldeard

39. The Queens
Anna McL Dabbs
40. Enterprise
Sue Hodgson

41. The Queens
Hilary Thurlow

42. Flower Basket
Joyce James

43. Machine-made Leaves
Hilary Thurlow

44. The Queens
Hilary Thurlow

45. Flower Trough
Hilary Thurlow

46. Potted Fern
Hilary Thurlow

47. The Queen's Entrance
Hilary Thurlow

Detail of the Hotel Metropole

49. Back View of Lady
TAG

50. Lady in Anorak
TAG

51. Lady in Brown
TAG

52. Small Person
TAG

53. Three People
TAG

54. Lady with Parcels
TAG

55. Man in Brown Suit
TAG

56. The Guildford Sign
Gina Day

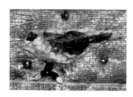

57. Small Bird

58. Lynx Train
Denise Teed (8.5hrs)

59. Guardian Exchange
Leslie Fallais

60. Samuel Taylors
Denise Teed

61. Bass Courtyard
Denise Teed

62. Arcade
Audrey Pidgeon (19.5hrs)

63. Metro Train
Edith Vertigan (79hrs)
64. Railway Bridge
Ruth Fowler (120hrs)
Charts by Alex Lloyd (120hrs)

65. Guardian Logos
Gina Day

66. Dorothy Perkins Logo
Audrey Pidgeon

67 Topshop Logo
Audrey Pidgeon

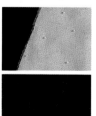

68. Sky
Kate Russell

Second Sun made by Mary Mawson

Enterprise

From mid-1993 to the end of 1994 the project had a series of empty shops or office spaces to use as a 'showroom' in the stunningly refurbished Victoria Quarter.

Kate designed displays for the shop windows using all the available press cuttings and photographs of work in progress. She put up large notices hoping to encourage shoppers and business people on lunch breaks to stop, look, call in and provide ideas for panel themes or elements to include on particular panels.

Pro Rege et Lege and the emerging designs for *Enterprise* and *Money Works* were all being constructed in the last and largest of the available spaces in the Quarter.

Variations on the theme of *Shopping* or the *City Centre* were often suggested by people as one of the key themes. Kate had already started a collection of photographs and had more or less decided to use the Queen Victoria Arcade which she thought would lend itself beautifully to embroidery. The inclusion of the arcade would not only represent an important architectural feature of Leeds but also be a gesture of thanks to John Bade, the Director of the Victoria Quarter.

There were no cash sponsors at this point but Kate knew that the Queen's Hotel and the Hotel Metropole would feature somewhere in appreciation of the Tapestry events they had agreed to sponsor.

One of the many visitors to the Tapestry 'showroom' was Tony Shelton from Leeds City Council's Centre Management Team. He was very positive about the idea of the Tapestry and was keen to participate in some way in the creation of a panel about the City Centre. He sent photographs, including a very dramatic shot of the Town Hall silhouetted against a darkening sky with the brightly lit big wheel of the Valentine's Fair. He also provided brochures and leaflets where Kate found a picture of Councillor John Trickett, leader of the Council, encouraging shoppers in Leeds to patronise the cafes. Tony talked about the Council's vision of a 24-hour city with pavement cafes and the changing face of the City Centre. He also arranged for the first sponsorship for the panel.

After this positive start progress on the panel floundered for a year or two. It took the retailers a lot longer to see the vision – in fact so long that they do not really feature in the panels. The only retailers represented here are Samuel Taylors Haberdashers, who provided all the nets used in the Tapestry and the stores represented by the clutch of shopping bags. All the stores, except Harvey Nichols who gave a small donation, were sponsored under the umbrella of the Burton Group (now Arcadia). Perhaps one day another panel will be made about a thriving, stylish and diverse shopping centre in which the majority of the major retailers

18.
Cllr John Trickett
Sheila Udakis

Photograph of the Valentine's Fair.

14.
Three Youths
Jackie Ford

60.
Samuel Taylors
Denise Teed

22.
Two
Ladies Eating
Freda Copley

13.
Lady in Red
Barbara Blacoe

8.
Three Shoppers
Textile Art Group

Metro Train
Ruth Fowler
Not used on the panel

and fashionable stores will be featured.

When Kate realised that the retailers in the Victoria Quarter were not going to be interested she looked further afield for sponsors, which is why the panel includes buildings from across the city centre and beyond.

Squeezing in a bridge with road and rail capabilities makes a rather awkward intercession. However, it did give Alex (then aged 13 years) son of Val Lloyd, an opportunity to be the first boy – in fact the only boy – to chart a design.

Vivienne Brown, Clare Bryan, Freda Copley, Jackie Ford, Sue and Sarah Hodgson, Denise Teed and Hilary Thurlow, all professional artists who have worked on *Enterprise*, also gave work-shops to encourage drawing, adventurous embroidery and the making of figures, leaves and flowers.

Many of the embroiderers involved in the project made beautiful and informative work sheets of their techniques. These were kept at the workshop and used by others of the volunteers who were in need of technical assistance. It is always amazing how so many textile artists are happy to share their skills for no reward except the joy of sharing. The next step is to include these sheets, with the author's permission, with other useful information about the project on a Leeds Tapestry website.

One of the pieces of embroidery, which is still a personal favourite of Kate's and many other people for the vitality and sense of humour it embodies, is *Two Ladies Eating* by Freda Copley.

"I did 20 hours a week for four years, starting at 5pm and often working until 10pm. Sometimes I would look up and discover it was two in the morning, so I would take it, on its frame, to bed with me and work on it a little bit more. I was so much in love with it! I would become totally absorbed. Sometimes I would go all Saturday and Sunday and just stitch. I would find myself getting more and more desperate to complete a piece and my fingers would fly faster and faster...."

Freda Copley

Another favourite on this panel is the sun embroidered by Mary Mawson. Although Mary had no formal training before she joined the Tapestry project, she is surely an artist. Her first sun, and first piece without using a chart, was so enchanting that when

Kate waxed lyrical about it, Mary made her another which is shown on page 122.

There are many other favourites. Most people find that the more you look the more there is to wonder at.

Freda, Sue, and Sarah were all available to help to construct this panel in the workshop at Armley Mills Museum. 'Construction' included the often laborious but very important task of 'finishing off' each section. Usually the details in the project brief given out with each section would instruct the volunteer to leave a piece unfinished.

The reason for this was because the exact shape may not necessarily be known, nor the size nor colour of the piece adjacent to it and a bit of extra fabric might be just what was needed. Sometimes a piece might need padding slightly to make it work and it may need re-positioning many times – sometimes quite radically.

Three or four people who know what they are looking at is the ideal – several people to pin, two to lift the panel up so the others can see how it looks and put it back on the trestles to adjust and stitch. The 'speckled granite' printed fabric was a real find in the market, and just right for the floor of *Enterprise* and the rich and glowing silks from James Hare were perfect for the sky, overlaid with nets to blend in the sun's rays. Adding the net shadows during the 'fine tuning' process was tricky but well worth it – they made the arcade and people really spring to life.

54.
Lady with Parcels
Textile Art Group

10.
Lady with Pushchair
Jackie Ford

20.
Man on stilts
Sarah Hodgson

Sun embroidered by Emi Clare, not used on the panel.

Money Works

1. Turkish Banknote

2. £50 English Banknote

3. Hungarian Banknote

Banknotes stitched by Anna McL Dabbs, Elsie Stockwell, Elizabeth Lancaster, Sue Wagstaff

4. Greek Banknote

5. 100 Portugese Escudos

6. £5 English Banknote
Angela Turner

7. 10,000 Italian Lire

8. Maltese Banknote

9. Israel Banknote

10. 100 Portugese Escudos

11. English £50 Banknote
Lesley Dove

12. Yorkshire Bank
Lizzie Ingle

13. 10,000 Italian Lire

14. Hungarian Banknote

15. Eastgate Chambers
Alicia Foster

16. Singer & Friedlander
Maureen Carr (20hrs)

17. NatWest Markets
Alicia Foster

18. Pannell House
Louise Pashley

19. Leeds & Holbeck
Edith Vertigan (205hrs)

All of the roofs were made in felt by Shani Tegerdine, charting by Sue Wagstaff, Pauline Idle, Alex Lloyd and Ann Wheatley

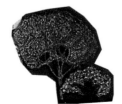

20. Trees
Lesley Dove

21. Tree

22. Tree
Denise Teed

23. KPMG Building
Dorothy Brown

24. Hambros Northern
Freda Copley

25. Tree
Denise Teed

26. Tree
Denise Teed

27.Tree
Denise Teed

28. Tree

29. Tree
Lesley Dove

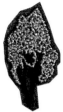

30. Tree
Denise Teed

31. Trees

32. Tree

33. Tree

34. Tree

Trees by Hilary Thurlow, Sue Geldeard and Davina Adams

35. Tree

36. Trees

37. Trees

38. Trees

39. Tree

40. Man with Jacket
Sue Geldeard

41. Lady with Pushchair
Janet Armstrong

42.Lady with Green Carrier
Denise Teed

43. Lady with Yellow Skirt
Janet Armstrong

44. Man with White Carrier
Janet Armstrong

45. Girl with Red Skirt
Janet Armstrong

46. Man in Suit
Anne Hobson

47. Walkng Man
Eileen Wilson

48. Man in Shirt Sleeves
Janet Armstrong

49. Man in Blue Suit
Sue Geldeard

50. Man with Newspaper
Sue Geldeard

51.Man with Phone
Denise Teed

52. Postman
Jackie Ford

53. Man with Red Braces
Sue Geldeard

54. Laura Ashley
Mary Mawson

55. Monsoon
Lynne Ward

56. Principles
Alicia Foster

57. Budget
Anna McL Dabbs

58. Country Casuals

59. Russell & Bromley
Ruth Fowler

60. Dorothy Perkins
Alicia Foster

61. House of Fraser
Lizzie Ingle

62. Top Man
Tracey Wood

63. Currys
Chris Birch

Charting for Charge cards by Val Lloyd, Pauline Idle, Ruth Fowler, Pauline Coates, Karen Howson, Sue Wagstaff

64. Dixon's
Chris Birch

65. Tandy
Alicia Foster

66. Harvey Nichols

67. Redmayne Bentley
Anna McL Dabbs

68. Debenhams
Angela Turner

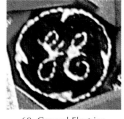

69. General Electrics
Lee Kerr

70. Share Prices
Alicia Foster

71. Wansbroughs
Clare Bryan & Lesley Dove

72. Fencing
Denise Teed

75 Window Catch by Edith
Vertigan
76. US Dollar (not used)
Lesley Dove

77. Letterhead by Gina Day
78. Turkish Banknote
(not used)

73. Halifax Letterhead
Gina Day

74. Aim
Gina Day

79. Leeds & Yorkshire Assurance
Lesley Dove & Gina Day

80. Yorkshire Enterprise
Denise Teed (3.5hrs)

81. Kwik Fit Card
Anna McL Dabbs

82. Pen
Joyce James

83. Piggy Bank
Gina Day

84. Fountain
Sue Hodgson

85. Owl
Freda Copley

86. Brown Dog
Barbara Gray

87. Black Dog
Barbara Gray

88. Star

89. Star

90. Star

91. Coins

92. Coins
Audrey Pigeon

93. Coins
Harriet Allen

94. Coins

95. Europe
Freda Copley (20hrs)

96. Hambros Northern
Sara Richards (5hrs)

97. KPMG
Angela Turner

98. Yorkshire Bank
Sara Richards (5hrs)

99. Deloitte & Touche

100. NatWest Marketing

101. Investors in People

102. Leeds & Holbeck
Merel Jackson

103. Sky
Freda Copley

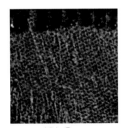

104. Grass
Hilary Thurlow

105. Cup, Saucer & Doily
Sue Hodgson & Audrey Pidgeon

Stitching sections on the panel.

14.
Hungarian Banknote

40.
Man with jacket
Sue Geldeard

Chris Birch's cross stitched piece not used on the panel.

In many ways the processes of producing this panel were similar to the making of *Pro Rege et Lege* which was begun almost a year earlier. It helped a great deal that some of the contacts were introduced to us by the sponsors of the first panel.

The financial services sector provided sponsorship for *Money Works* over a relatively short period of time (late 1993-96). This was achieved due to the sector being a relatively self-contained, and therefore more easily identifiable, community.

The sponsors involved in consultation wanted similar things - images of Head Offices, or the Leeds Branch of the organisation or illustrations of the products of their business. At a meeting Kate had with the Directors of GE Capital they brought out their annual reports and marketing brochures but it was their store charge cards which interested her most. They were colourful, recognisable to the general public and would be interesting to reproduce visually.

As further consultations with the sector continued through 1994, three distinct design ideas became clear. The first - Leeds based buildings; the second - objects which represented the various business transactions and finally - global financial transactions. From the design point of view this presented a problem; how could these be shown in one unified whole? Kate still is not sure how well the finished result works and whether or not the illusion she tried to create is apparent. In the foreground is a desk with money box, coffee cup, paper work and pen. Through the window is Park Square with financial sector buildings around the perimeter and in the sky above a rather eurocentric view of the earth surrounded by coins and banknotes of various currencies.

Inspiration, energy and enjoyment were very much to the fore during the first three or four years when the volunteers gathered weekly at Kate's home and studio in Chapel Allerton.

The only real disappointment experienced during the making of this panel was that Chris Birch's excellent embroidery of the Leeds & Holbeck building could not be used. The sponsors preferred a perspective view of their building incorporating the front door. Fortunately Edith Vertigan was ready to take on the task with her usual speed. Chris's piece has certainly not been wasted though, it has been taken to exhibitions, talks and demonstrations for the last seven years as an example of one of the many techniques available for new recruits.

In order to get the banknotes colour copied and printed onto fabric permission had to be sought from the Bank of England. We were asked to make the notes a different size from the originals presumably to avoid supermarkets being swamped with embroidered currency. They were the talking point of the panel; people could not believe they had been stitched and always marvelled at the quality and delicacy of the embroidery. In spite of the obvious eye-strain,

the needlewomen must have enjoyed the task and many came back for more. This resulted in more notes being made than used even after Kate had managed to find a place for some on the desk. Now we see the wisdom from the Bank of England. Along with Chris's building, the spares await the *Serendipity* panel.....because they are too big to spend.

Various elements were introduced to add a touch of lightness and humour to what threatened to be a rather serious image. These included the bright red piggy bank, raised work cup, saucer and pen (authentic images as photographed on a desk at the London Stock Exchange in Leeds), as well as the grey felt roofs, made by Shani Tegerdine, which converted most of the buildings into money boxes.

Similarly the use of Park Square with its statue of Circe was designed to bring greenery, life and people to the panel rather than geographical accuracy of placement of the buildings , though two of them are in the right environs.

Only one of the figures represents an actual person. The 'Man with Red Braces' (53) is Richard Kempner, husband of Gillian Holding and both from Addleshaw Booth. Gillian is both a volunteer and a Trustee of the Tapestry and one of several embroiderers for whom working on the project was the catalyst for a career change.

The decision, in 1992, to begin a feasibility study into making a Millennium Tapestry was based partly on the knowledge Kate had gained from the Leeds Common Purpose Programme in 1992/93. It became clear to her that Leeds is the country's second city for Law and Finance and that part of the reason for this is that the sectors work closely together. This, she felt, should be echoed in the designs of the panels by placing them next to each other in the overall scheme and with some visual links. Originally the idea was to run through the spectrum of colours in the background fabrics of the panels. As titles changed or sections were amalgamated or simply abandoned due to lack of interest and the number of panels shrank from twenty four to twenty to eighteen and finally to sixteen, this idea was gradually diluted. It exists now as the colour strips on the sides of the postcards and in the books. Maybe one day, when the panels have a permanent home, they could be re-framed with these colours in the mounts.

50.
Man with newspaper
Sue Geldeard

As the first two of the originally intended twenty four panels, *Money Works* and *Pro Lege et Rege* have similar background colours. They also share similarities in design; the earth in place of the Leeds Coat of Arms, the buildings in a similar scale and position and the documents, charters and certificates in the foreground. The charge certificate with the border of decorative shields appears on both panels.

24.
Hambros Northern
Freda Copley

This panel was a joy to put together. Assisted by Freda Copley, Sue and Sarah Hodgson on the design and construction side and a whole host of cheerful stitchers, there was a great deal of laughter in the Burling and Mending room at Armley Mills and plenty of tea and biscuits to restore energy. All the problems of the world, not just the financial sector, were resolved as needles and tongues worked together in close harmony.

23.
KPMG Building
Dorothy Brown

Pro Rege et Lege

1. Small Owl
Audrey Gabbitas

2. Large Owls
Audrey Gabbitas

3. Walker Morris
Val Lloyd (210hrs)

5. Lamb
Colleen Nicoll

4. Leeds Magistrates Court by Sarah Hodgson

6. Ribbon
K Russell & Sue Hodgson

7. Helmet & Plume
Anne Darch

8. Hammond Suddards
Lizzie Ingle

9. Read Hind Stewart
Denise Williams & Alicia Foster

10. Simpson Curtis
Anne Darch

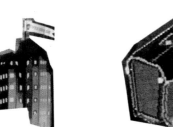

11. Booth & Co
Clare Bryan

12. BRP Man
Carol Cook(10hrs)

13. Lady in Blue
Carol Cook (10hrs)

14. Lady in Green
Carol Cook(10hrs)

15. Leeds Magistrates Court
Lesley Fallais

16. Eversheds
Sara Richards & F Copley

17. Briefcase
Sara Richards

18. Police & Defendant
Perry Mason & Rachel Ingle

19. Dibb Lupton Broomhead
Sarah Pattison

20. Law Society
Glynis Evans & Anne Darch

21. Grahame Stowe Bateson
Lizzie Ingle

22. Three Judges
Sue Hodgson (52hrs)

23. Computer
Kate Russell

24. Two Judges
Gillian Holding

25. The Jury
Sarah Hodgson

Simpson Curtis

26. Bridewell Switchboard
Margaret Smith

27. Walker Morris
Mary Mawson, Rachel Ingle
(Two embroidered)

28. Ford & Warren
Freda Copley

29. Girl in Pink
Freda Copley

30. Charge Certificate
Susan & Valerie Wagstaff

31. Judge's Cloth
Lesley Dove

32. Lupton Fawcett
Sarah Hodgson

33. Planning & Compensation
Sarah Hodgson & Lesley Dove

34. Bridewell Charter
Shirley Whitley

35. Rat
Colleen Nicoll & Sarah Hodgson

Collage for design of the panel
Kate Russell

36. Booth & Co
Cathy Clarke

37. Old Bridewell
S Richards & C Birch

38. Eversheds
Louise Pashley

Charting and needlepoint for three sets of books by Avril Bellwood, Chris Birch (53hrs), Carole Evans, Glynis Evans, Alicia Foster (30hrs) and Susan Wagstaff

41. Bookcase (lower left)
Freda Copley

43. Criminal Law Book
Linda M Hill

11.
Booth & Co
Clare Bryan

The research and fund-raising for this panel began in concert with the feasibility study in January 1993. The contacts Kate had made during the Common Purpose Programme helped enormously and the majority of people she spoke to expressed an interest not only in sponsoring a representation of their business but also becoming involved in the overall design and stitching of the Legal Sector Panel.

These discussions led by various routes to the Law Society, professional journals, Barristers Chambers, Legal Aid, the Police and The Magistrates Court and eventually to all the aspects of Law in action which are illustrated on the panel.

2.
Large Owls
Audrey Gabbitas

The first full-scale design was shown at one of the lunch time gatherings hosted by Booth & Co and organised by Shabnam Qasim, a solicitor, in 1993. Shabnam was one of the original enthusiasts of the Tapestry project, even when there was nothing to see, and became involved in all aspects of design and production. As with most of the other twenty or so legal professionals who volunteered to work on the

15.
Leeds Magistrates Court
Lesley Fallais

embroidery, she discovered that her job was too demanding to allow sufficient time and energy to learn new skills in order to embroider projects. In due course she became one of three who gave up their careers in Law for more artistic pursuits.

The events at Booth & Co were a form of 'in kind' sponsorship which has been repeated regularly during the making of the panels. Employees from other legal firms attended and in due course it was clear from their enthusiasm that the twenty-four panel project was feasible. They offered sponsorship and to become involved with design consultation and embroidering. The fact that the launch was under the auspices of one of the top legal firms in Leeds gave it credibility and much needed publicity.

The first section to be stitched was the *Three Judges* chosen for the express purpose of providing a tangible and sensory glimpse of the quality of the embroidery envisaged for the Tapestry. Sue Hodgson, who made the piece, was introduced to the project when Kate gave a talk about it to the Yorkshire Branch of the Embroiderers' Guild in

February 1993 during the feasibilty study period. Sue is a professional embroiderer whose raised or stumpwork seemed an ideal medium for the archetypal image of the three judges. When the piece was complete Kate took it with her to meetings with legal sector firms, raising awareness, funds and often a smile.

From the outset the intention was to make each panel an authentic impression of the sector to be represented. This meant that sometimes less obvious features were highlighted. Many hours were spent tracking down female members of the Judiciary, until Kate approached the then Recorder of Leeds, his Honour Judge David Savill QC, who put her in touch with Judges Linda Sutcliffe and Jacqueline Davies, two very enthusiastic women who had been called to the bar together. It was not possible to photograph them in court so they generously arranged to have a photo shoot at Linda's home. The Tapestry portrays one of them in full ceremonial dress which is worn when a judge is sworn in at the House of Lords. It is also worn at other

ceremonial occasions such as the Westminster Abbey service at the beginning of the legal year. The other is wearing bench robes used in the Crown Court.

22.
Three Judges
Sue Hodgson (52hrs)

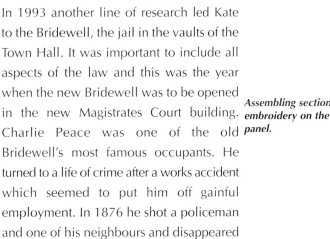

24.
Two Judges
Gillian Holding

Assembling sections of embroidery on the panel.

On the trail of a suitable image to represent Law in Education Kate met Professor Brian Hogan from Leeds University at the Town Hall Tavern (the Tapps). Despite the many stories he told she could not visualise any of it on the panel and eventually chose one of his text books to represent understanding the Law. Shortly after this meeting Professor Hogan died and his widow was thoughtful enough to let us know how much it meant to her that the embroidery is a permanent memento of his career.

In 1993 another line of research led Kate to the Bridewell, the jail in the vaults of the Town Hall. It was important to include all aspects of the law and this was the year when the new Bridewell was to be opened in the new Magistrates Court building. Charlie Peace was one of the old Bridewell's most famous occupants. He turned to a life of crime after a works accident which seemed to put him off gainful employment. In 1876 he shot a policeman and one of his neighbours and disappeared

25.
The Jury
Sarah Hodgson

34.
Bridewell Charter
Shirley Whitley

44.
Sky
Freda Copley

from Sheffield for several years until someone recognised him in London and he was sent to Leeds Assizes.

By April 1995, when the project moved from Kate's kitchen to Armley Mills, the final design for this panel (mark 4) was more or less established. The majority of sections had been stitched onto the silk backing cloth, itself backed with a strong calico to take the weight of all the raised work. The silk had been previously overdyed with indigo hot water dye in a large stainless steel bucket on the cooker; dip dyeing to make the colour darker at the bottom, fading towards the top to lend a sense of *gravitas* to the panel.

The arrival of each newly completed piece of embroidery was always a thrill and never more so than on this the first panel when none of us knew if it would turn out as we had hoped. When the Bridewell Charter arrived and was carefully unfolded from the protective tissue paper there was a gasp - it looked so much like a scroll of parchment - and almost bated breath as it

was put into position on the panel. Shirley Whitley had moved from Leeds during the making of this piece and so had not managed to bring it to the workshop regularly to assess the ever-changing visual relationships between one piece and another. In this particular instance it was a delightful surprise, adding just the right amount of movement in three dimensions in that part of the panel.

There are many volunteers who contributed to the creation of a panel whose work is not easily seen nor acknowledged. For example those who would finish off sections of embroidery in readiness for 'stitching-down' by turning in the edges or maybe adding a strip of colour to fill a gap. When someone needed a break from the often back-aching work of bending and reaching over a panel to stitch, they might sit for a while and 'finish off', allowing another to take their place stitching on the panel.

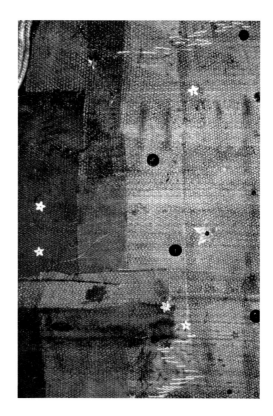

Then there were those who did the 'charting'. Dozens of people, many tutored in their craft by Val Lloyd, designed a graph showing what colour and where to make each stitch. Val Lloyd did the first chart of the project for the 'Criminal Law book' (43) which took 61 hours. Sometimes, with an intricate chart, it would take longer to draw than to stitch.

On this panel the other 'charters' include Pauline Coates, Chris Birch, Pauline Idle, Lee Kerr, Sara Richards and Susan and Valerie Wagstaff.

The 'fine-tuning'; blending and harmonising with nets, french knots, beads and other stitchery and applique was a lengthy job on this our first completed work. On the eve of the unveiling stitching went on until the Museum closed.

The Hotel Metropole had agreed to host the celebration of the first panel's completion as in-kind sponsorship and held a breakfast event. Timed to capture the biggest possible audience of legal professionals it also

Cross-stitch chart for "Criminal Law" by Smith & Hogan designed by Val Lloyd (61hrs)

Criminal Law Book

43.
Criminal Law Book
Linda Smith

attracted the Lord Mayor, councillors and officers of Leeds City Council, volunteers existing and new, potential sponsors and friends. Many of those attending would stay with the project through the seven more years it would take to complete the panels. Woman's Hour, as well as local press, turned out to interview Kate and other volunteers plus the two honourable judges who, with a witty and congratulatory speech, unveiled the panel. It was gratifying for those who had worked on the embroidery to hear the gasp of wonder and disbelief and to see the faces of those crowding round the panel for a closer look.

3.
Walker Morris
Val Lloyd (210hrs)

The unveiling of Pro Rege et Lege, 1995

Volunteer Embroiderers

Davina Adams
Jane Adams
June Adams
Nell Adams
Diane Allott
Patricia Andrews
Brenda Archer
Janet Armstrong
Mrs Armstrong
Jean Atkinson
Claire Balchin
Daphne Balchin
Roberta Balmforth
Jennifer Barber
Ann Barker
Judith Baron
Jackie Barron
Mrs Olive Beech
Bridget Beer
William Beer
Avril Bellwood
Betty Bertrand
Elizabeth Bidgood
Barbara Blacoe
Joan Bogunovic
Margaret Booth
Anne Boyle
Sue Braithwaite
Kath Bretherick
Ann Brown
Dorothy Brown
Elizabeth Brown
Jan Brown
Patricia Brown
Vivienne Brown
Yvonne Brownett
Clare Bryan
May Burns
Muriel Butt
Janet Carding
Maureen Carr
Margaret Chambers
Celia Charnley
Emi Clare
Ann Clark
Judith Clark
Margaret Clark
Cathy Clarke
Pauline Clayden
Marion Cole
Carol Cook
Gill Cook
Mary Cook
Julia Cooper
Freda Copley
Margaret Cordell
Anne Cove
Rita Cox
Sylvia Crowther
Eileen Cummings

Rosemary Cysarz
Anna McL Dabbs
Anne Darch
Renee Davidson
Catherine Davies
Patricia Davies
Mrs M Dawes
Pauline Dean
Jane Dew
Rita Dobson
Alda C Don
Veronica Dore
Arshima Dost
Ayesha Dost
Lesley Dove
Caroline Dunn
Ena Dunn
Sheila Eagleton
Marion Eddolls
Freda Ellis
Maureen Elvidge
Glynis Evans
Sue Evans
Sheila Exley
Lesley Fallals
Barbara Farrugia
Liz Firth
Mary Fletcher
Alicia Foster
Ruth Fowler
Marjorie Fox
Margaret Foxcroft
Ann Francis
Audrey Gabbitas
Muriel Gabbitas
Shirley Gale
Joan Gamble
Judith Gamble
Enid Gator
Sue Geldeard
Eileen Gibb
Hanni Gill
Mavis Glenn
Mandy Gomersall
Val Gomersall
Sue Gough
Janet Grainger
Barbara Gray
Maggie Grey
Hannah (Wigton Moor)
Jean Hardman
June Hardy
Countess of Harewood
Rosemary Hargreaves
Sue Hargreaves
Godfrey Harland
Vera Harrington
Beverley Harvey
Sheila Haughton
Margaret Haynes

Barbara Hebden
Laura Hebden
Mrs Hedley
Brenda Heffer
Linda Hill
Lynn Hill
Marjory Hill
Maureen Hindes
Anne Hobson
Sarah Hodgson
Sue Hodgson
Betty Hoggart
Joan Holah
Gillian Holding
Sally Holmes
Freda Hooper
Val Horner
Karen Howson
Olive Hudson
Margaret Hulme
Julie Hyde
Pauline Idle
Lizzie Ingle
Rachel Ingle
Brian Jackson
Cynthia Jackson
Judith Jackson
Merel Jackson
Joyce James
Marian C Jenner
Rosie Kearton
Mildred Keedy
Marie Kell
Margaret Kenny
Valerie Kent
Lee Kerr
Margaret Kingston
Mary Kingston
Mrs Kirby
Pamela Kirby
Ann Kirk
Florence Kirk
Mr J Kirk
Barbara Kitson
Cllr Brenda Lancaster
Elizabeth Lancaster
Joan Langfield
Ruth Lawrence
Susan Lawton
Betty Laycock
Catherine Lee
Jean Lewis
Sallie Lindley
Joan Lister
Victoria Littlewood
Val Lloyd
Evi Malm
Thelma Manning
Jack Marlowe
Ann Marshall

Carol Marshall
Angela Mason
Mrs Mason
BS "Perry" Mason
Mary Mawson
Beryl Mayhew
Joyce Maynard
Jenny McLean
Mary Mellor
Mollie Midgley
Margaret Milne
June Mitton
Zuber Mohammed
Mark (Wigton Moor)
Auriol Moore
Jackie Moore
Joan Moore
Mary Needleman
Mrs Newby
Jean Nichols
Colleen Nicoll
Jan Oddy
Monica Parnaby
Helen Parrott
Louise Pashley
Valorie Patillo
Karen Pattison
Sarah Pattison
Mrs Peel
Audrey Pidgeon
Christine Pitchfork
Judy Poole
Pat Potton
Olwen Poulter
Hazel Rand
Judith Reynolds
Gloria Rhodes
Sara Richards
Chris Richardson
Mrs Richardson
Veronica Robson
Mrs Jill Rothwell
Kay Royce
Kate Russell
Victoria Russell
Jill Rutter
Jacky Ryder
Mary Sanders
Kathy Schofield
Vivienne Scott
Ruth Seaman
Helen Sedgewick
Mrs AM Sharpe
Shirley Shaw
Cynthia Shipley
Beverley Silverman
Renee Silverman
Archana Singh
Jean Sinister
Sheila Slater

Beryl Smith
Linda Smith
Margaret Smith
Mary Smith
Pat Smith
Sheila Smith
Maureen Spearing
Cath Stewart
Rosalind Stirk
Elsie Stockwell
June Stockwell
Vicky Storr
Judith Sugden
Mrs Sutcliffe
Sandra Sutton
Sylvia Tancock
Diane Taylor
Janet Taylor
Jean Taylor
Karen Taylor
Denise Teed
Shani Tegerdine
Elizabeth Thackrah
Mrs Thirlwell
Liz Thompson
Hilary Thurlow
Susan Timlin
Barbara Town
Margaret Turnbull
Angela Turner
Myra Turner
Sheila Udakis
Edith Vertigan
Kathryn Vincent
Verna Wadelin
Valerie Wagstaff
Barbara Walker
Jessica Walker
Vi Walker
Sally Walton
Hazel Ward
Lynne Ward
Jean Webber
Jan Webster
Janet Wenham
Marie Whaley
Ann Wheatley
Shirley Whitley
Claire Wildman
Jackie Wilkinson
Denise Williams
Carol Wilson
Eileen Wilson
Anne Winteler
Tracey Wood
Minnie Woodward
Gwen Woolliscroft
Ann Wragg
Dorothy Wrench
Carol Wurr
Susan Wagstaff

Volunteer Groups

Bramley Community Centre
CHALCS
CHEL
Churwell Youth Centre

Dosti
Fibre Optics FX
Getaway Girls
Hey Days
Hooner Kelah

Leeds Environmental Forum
Leeds Racial Harassment
Lincoln Green Youth Base
Mandela Centre
Milan Centre

Refuge Action Leeds
Scott Hall Residents Association
Sikh Temple Ladies Group
Swarthmore Education Centre
The Carnival Committee

Vera Media
Vietnamese Community Association
Voluntary Action Leeds
Womens Health Matters
Yorkshire Womens Theatre Co

Other Volunteers

Zahir Ahmed
Charlotte Allan
Harriett Allan
Peggy Allen
Mr Allott
Barbara Alloyd
Usmah Almas
Lorna Arblaster
Betty Archer
Kate Ascott
Sheila Ash
John Ashbee
Lucy Aspinall
May Aspinall
Cllr Bernard Atha
Jacov Atik
Joy Atkinson
Patricia Atkinson
Jean Ayling
Penny Babbington
Stuart Baker
Jocelyn Baldwin
Sue Ball
Julie Ballantyne
Jacquie Banks
Martin Banks
Andrew Bannister
Hilda Bareham
D Bartle
Angela Bates
Isobel Bayliss
Cllr Malcolm Bedford
Bridgett Bedham
Ruth Bell
Fauzia Bhatti
Christine Birch
Cllr Judith Blake
Pat Bloor
Gail Bolland
Audrey Bolton
Mark Bowles
Elizabeth Bowling
Rosemary Bradley
Mrs Bradshaw
Anne Branch
Peter Brears
Vega Brennan
Liz Brightwell
Deborah Britton
Hazel Britton
Jacquie Brookfield
Mrs Pauline Brooks
Cllr Jonathon Brown
Christine Buckley
Chris Buckton
Rob Bumby
D Burns
Elizabeth Cadd
Chris Calow
Judith Calvert
Edna Carr
Mary Carrington
Tracy Carroll
Pat Cartledge
Alan Carver
Cllr Ann Castle
Helen Caukwell
Margaret Chalmers
Olive Chamberlain
Fiona Chapel
Eve Charing
Alun Chisnall
Sister B Clarey
Dinah Clark
Don Clark
Cynthia Clarke
Deborah Clayton
Mrs A Coates
Mrs Pauline Coates

Andy Cole
Sheila Cole
Mrs MJ Coleman
Peter Connelly
Paula Convy
Penny Cookson
Shirley Cooper
Muriel Cork
Peter Cowgill
Pauline Cowie
Elizabeth Cowling
Barbara Creswell
Anne Croft
Shirley Crosby
Edward Crow
Anne Crowther
Linda Crozier
Helka Czuhra
Jane Daguerre
Anne Darwin
Judge Jacqueline Davies
Mrs M Davies
Gina Day
Jean Daybell
Carole Dexter
Mr Dobson
Sue Donnelly
Robin Dove
Helen Driscoll
Jamie from Drummonds
Gordon Dunn
Nell Dunn
Mrs Sue Dutton
Mabel Duxbury
Allan Dyer
Joan Dyer
Hilary Dyson
Patricia Egan
Joan Elliott
Margaret Ellis
Winnie Ellis
Mrs Ellison
Moira Emmett
Mrs P England
Carole Evans
Mrs Fairburn
Jenny Fairlee
Val Firth
Mrs Sue Fishburn
Avtaar Flora
Jackie Ford
Margaret Ford
Cllr Michael Fox
M Fraser
Danny Freeman
John Gabbitas
Jennifer Gallagher
Mrs Garrard
Alan Garth
Al Garthwaite
Enid Gates
Judy Gaunt
Gillian Gaynor
Lea Geldeard
Kate Genever
Ravinder Ghir
Elaine Gillett
Christine Goodall
Kevin Grady
Muriel Greaves
Karen Green
Jackie Haggar
Susan Haigh
June Hall
Jennifer Hallam
Sylvia Hargreaves
Vivien Harper
Nina Hawkins
Jean Healey

Joyce Heaton
Kath Heaton
Florinda Henderson
Liz Herbert
Mary Herbert
Margaret Hill
Mick Hill
Denise Hirschman
Mrs Hodgson
Ray Holah
Sylvia Hold
Brenda Holding
Mrs Holmes
Jean Holroyd
Gill Holt
Jenny Horam
Sheila Houghton
A Howes
Gwen Howgate
Mrs Huby
Cllr David Hudson
Aveline Hume
Inder Hunjan
Yasmin Hussein
Jane Hustwit
Christine Maclean
Hutchins
Julie Ann Ickeringill
Pauline Idle
Cllr Mohammed Iqbal
Pam Irish
Olive Jackson
Ann Jacques
Barbara Johnson
Liz Johnson
Sandie Johnson
Mike Jolly
Patricia Jones
V Jones
Jafwant Jutta
Gill Kay
Gill Keddie
Richard Kempner
Sue Kershaw
Martin Key
Helen King
Margaret Kitson
Carolyn Knaggs
Eileen Knighton
Alwyn Knowles
Ruksana Kwaja
Cllr Graham Latty
Linda Lawrence
Ann Lawson
Ann Lea
Kathryn Lee
Kelly Light
Connie Lightfoot
Alex Lloyd
Carolyn Lord
Keith Loudon
John Lydon
Jessica Macdonald
Karam Macdonald
Margaret Macdonald
Catriona Mackintosh
Lillibet Mackintosh
Jenny Maclean
Susan Maens
Cllr Abdul Malik
Hannah Malkin
Paul Malkin
Barbara Marsh
Elizabeth Marshall
Eric Marshall
Nicki Martineaux
Anne Matthews
Jim McArthur
Jill McCaudlish

Lynn McCuish
Julie McHale
Stephen McHugh
Amish McMahon
Josie Medved
Veronica Metcalf
Sonya Middleton
Mr Milne
Brenda Milner
Cllr Liz Minkin
Cllr Marian Monks
John Moore
John Morgan
Margaret Morrish
Katie Moses
Mervyn Msaga
Beryl Murray
Darren Newby
Michael J O'Donell
Mary O'Regan
Sheila Overton
Eileen Page
Noleen Park
Stephen Park
Cheryl Parker
Brian Peace
Elsie Peace
Freda Pearce
Mary Penberthy
Jean Pick
Helen Pickering
Susan Pitter
Elizabeth Pollard
Denise Preston
Gyandharm Pring
Eileen Pullam
Shabnam Qasim
Mrs Joyce Ratcliff
Chris Ratcliffe
Alison Ravetz
Josephine Rawling
Rosalind Rawson
Mark Rawstron
Louise Read
Valerie Redmire
Pauline Reeve
Dorothy Renshaw
David Rhodes
Dalvier Riat
Bev Rice
Gill Richardson
Shaun Richardson
Sheila Richardson
G. Riggs
Kathy Robertson
Jed Robinson
Shelagh Robinson
Ana Rodriquez
Pam Roe
Mickey Roo
Daru Rooke
Brenda Rose
Mollie Rosenhead
Miss E Rowland
Tricia Ryan
I Sandor
Elaine Van Sante
Leo Seaton
Alison Selkirk
M Shackleton
Beth Shaw
Tony Shelton
Leslie Shilling
Eric Simpson
Mrs Simpson
Moira Sloan
Gillian Smallwood
Cynthia Smith
Doreen Smith

Helen Smith
Jean Snowball
Maria Spellacy
Alison Stansfield
Clifford Stead
Tamara Stein
Mrs E Stephens
Penny Stephenson
Kirsti Stindale
Pauline Stone
Jane Stringer
Olivia Stross
Lynne Strutt
Cllr Linda Sullivan
Jean Summer
Philip Sumner
Anna Sutcliffe
Carol Sutcliffe
Judge Linda Sutcliffe
Pat Suttle
Jane Sykes
Mary Tate
Charlotte Taylor
Marjorie Taylor
Jane Tessyman
Hilary Thackray
M Thornber
Geoffrey Thornton
Muriel Thorp
Sandra Thorpe
Ursula Thorpe
Debbie Tiffany
Sally Timmins
Christine Toogood
Julie Townend
Tim Vernon
Doreen Waclawiak
Susan Wagstaff
Ann Walker
Connie Walker
Jean Walker
Joan Walker
Julie Walker
Robin Walker
Tina Walker
Sandra Wallace
Sian Wallace
Ivy Walton
Shannon Wan
William Warner
Roger Watkins
Jean Watson
Serena Watson
Nick Wayne
Caroline Webb
Andy Welch
Jan Wells
Lynda Wilcock
Emma Wilkinson
Laura Wilkinson
Paul Wilkinson
Brian Wilson
D Wilson
Donald Wilson
Joan Wilson
Peter Wilson
Jan Wood
Lesley Wood
Nick Wood
Mrs Janis Woodcock
Sara Woods
Barbara Wright
John Wybor
Maria Young
Pamela Young
Susan Zito
James Brown
Patricia Lynch
Pat Wilson

Donors

Major Donors

Anonymous
Barclays Bank plc
Countess of Harewood
Elida Faberge
Evans of Leeds plc
Hopkins Catering Equipment

Leeds TEC
Lloyds TSB
Millennium Festival Fund
Olav Arnold Trust
Peter Moores Foundation
The National Lottery through The Arts Council of England

Donors

Betty Bertrand
Mr & Mrs Bousfield
Kathleen Bretherick
Alderman Vyvyan Cardno
Peter & Sylvia Crowther
Judge Jacqueline Davies
Edwin Woodhouse Trust
George Martin Trust
Dennis Herbert
Mary Herbert
Mrs Ann Hollingworth
Alice Hopkins

Cllr David Hudson
Mrs Gillian Hudson
Denise Jagger
James Johnson
Cllr Brenda Lancaster
Cllr E & Mr L Minkin
Kate & Brian Peace
Susan Pitter
Ms S Richardson
Scurrah Wainwright Trust
Judge Linda Sutcliffe
Alan Talbot

Sponsors

Abbey Holford Rowe
Academy Restaurant
June Adams
Adel Parochial Church Council
Age Concern Leeds
Ainsleys Bakers
Aireborough Gilbert & Sullivan Society
Airedale Air Conditioning
Albert Farnell
Alwoodley Golf Club
Alwoodley Park Church
Anon for Cllr E Minkin
Anon for Leeds/Bradford Airport
Arcadia plc (Burton Group)
Archbold Freightage Ltd
E J Arnold Trust
Asda plc
Ashfield Nursing Homes
Association of Secretaries
Association of Women Graduates
Cllr Bernard Atha
B & N Group
Baptist Church
Barclays Bank plc
Barlow Refractory Products
Mrs Judith Baron
Barr Wallace Arnold
Barristers Chambers, 9 Woodhouse Square
Bartlett & Co Ltd
Bass North plc
Mrs A Bates
Justine Beak
Bernina Knitting Club
Elizabeth Bidgood
Birse Construction plc
Bishop of Ripon
Sue Blackwell
Cllr Blake (WISE)

Boys Brigade
Barbara Taylor Bradford
Brahma Kumaris Group
Bramhope Parish Council
Brethericks
Brewster Bye
British Judo Association
British Professional Women
British Telecom
British Waterways
David Brotherton
HE & FJ Brown Ltd
Alfred Brown Ltd
Bryan & Co
Mrs Audrey Burton
C & A
Alderman Vyvyan Cardno
Care Homes Association
Carl Bro Group
Carlsberg Tetley
Carlton & Stainbeck Surgeries
Carnegie College
Chapel Allerton Lawn Tennis & Squash Club
Jack Charlton
Chartered Institute of Environmental Health
Christian Science Churches
City Centre Churches
City Link
Clariant plc
Classic Cars
Clayton Walker
The Clothworkers Foundation
Co Ventures
College of Music
Common Purpose (Jane Hustwit)
Company Cars Ltd

Concord
COLECT
Co-operative Bank plc
Coutts Bank
Cranswick Watson, Solicitors
Sylvia Crowther
Dacre Son and Hartley
Damond Lock Grabowski
Jean Daybell
Deloitte Touche
Dibb Lupton
Ayesha Dost
F & C Drake of Golcar
Drapers Company
Drawn Metal Ltd
DTZ (Debenham Tie Leung Ltd)
Duttons for Buttons
Electromec Access
Englafot Construction Ltd
English Sports Council
Environment Agency
Evans of Leeds plc
Eversheds
Eye on the Aire
Federation of Small Businesses
Ford & Warren
John & Annabelle Forrest
Foxwood Mount Residential Home
Foyle & Kirk
Friends of Leeds Grammar School
Friends of Leeds Museum
Fulneck School
G E Capital
Joan Gamble
Gardening Which
Garforth Community College
Gateways School
Geofabrics

George Martin Trust
Girls Brigade
GNER
Goddard Wybor Practice
Mrs Gosnay
Gosnays Sports Agency
Grahame Stowe Bateson
Granary Wharf
Gregory Properties
Grimley International Properties
Grove Methodist Church, Horsforth
Guardian Insurance
Guiseley Gilbert and Sullivan Society
Haleys Hotel
Halifax plc
Hambros Bank
Hammond Suddards
Harewood Arms Hotel
Harewood Estate
Harewood House Trust
Harvey Nichols & Co Ltd
Headingley Amateur Operatics
Headingley Hall
Henderson Insurance Brokers
Mary Herbert
Tony Hesselwood
Jack Higgins
Hollingworth and Moss
Holy Trinity Church
Hopkins Catering Equipment
HSBC
I Too project
Cllr Illingworth
Inner Wheel Club of Leeds
Intake Arts College
Brian & Merel Jackson
Jarvis Parkway Hotel & Country Club
Jarvis Porter Group

Sponsors

JCS Motor Repairs
Johnson Radley
Joseph Rowntree Trust
Jubilee 2000
Kidney Patients Association (LGI)
Freda Kirk
KPMG
Cllr Graham Latty(MICE)
Lawnswood Dental Care
Lax & Shaw
Leeds & Holbeck Building Society
Leeds Amateur Operatics
Leeds Art Collection Fund
Leeds Benevolent Society for Single Ladies
Leeds Care Homes Association
Leeds Church Institute
Leeds City Centre Management Initiative
Leeds City Council
Leeds City Council Highways Department
Leeds City Council, Millennium Committee
Leeds City Council, Centenary Committee
Leeds City Council, Community Chest
Leeds City Council, Art@Leeds
Leeds Civic Trust
Leeds College of Music
Leeds Co-operative Society
Leeds County Guides
Leeds Dental Institute
Leeds Dyers Company
Leeds Environment City Partnership
Leeds Express
Leeds Federation of Townswomens Guilds
Leeds Gilbert and Sullivan Society
Leeds Girls High School
Leeds Golf Club
Leeds Grammar School
Leeds Health Authority
Leeds Hospital Fund
Leeds International Pool
Leeds International Rotary Club
Leeds Junior Chamber of Commerce
Leeds Kirkgate Markets Office
Leeds Metropolitan University
Leeds Rhinos
Leeds Rotary Club International
Leeds Skyrack Express
Leeds Swordfish Appeal
Leeds Teaching Hospitals
Leeds Training Trust
Leeds Tuesday Luncheon Club
Leeds United AFC
Leeds Voice
Leeds Voluntary & Community Sector Initiative
Leeds Womens Luncheon Club
Phillipa Lesta
Lex Transfleet

London Stock Exchange
Lord Harewood Trust
Keith Loudon
Lupton Fawcett
John Lydon
Lynx Express Ltd
Misses Mackintosh
Marks and Spencer
Martin House Hospice
McCourt Newton
Monsignor Peter McGuire
Meanwood Urban Valley Farm
Kay Mellor
Mencap Leeds
Merrion Hotel
Metanoics
The Methodist Church
Methodist Homes
Methodist Homes for the Aged
Metro Leeds
Midland Bank plc
Midland Mainline
Cllr E Minkin (MICE)
MKC Limited
Moor Allerton Golf Club
Mrs Pat Moore
Moorlands School
Moortown Golf Club
Moravian Church
Morgan Properties
John Morgan
Margaret Morrish
Miss Pamela Moses
Mothers Union
National Heart Research Fund
National Trust
Natwest Bank plc
Natwest Markets
Network for Successful UK Women
New Working Ways
NHS
Northern Lights
Northern Spirit
Norwich Union
NSPCC
Ntl (Cable & Wireless)
Nuffield Institute of Health
Nurses League
One Stop Architects
Open College Network
Opp2K
Ove Arup
Gwyneth Owen
Oxford Place Methodist Mission
Pannell Kerr Forster
Park Lane College
Parton Products

Douglas Pask
Paul Hinds Solicitors
Peacock & Sons
Pinsent Curtis
Susan Pitter
Pool Court at 42 The Calls
Price Waterhouse Cooper
Principles
Privilege Insurance
Deborah Protter
Pudsey Rambling Club
Quakers
Queens Hotel
Radiant Health Foundation
Railtrack
Mrs P Rakusen
Read Hind Stewart
Redmayne Bentley
Regional Railway NE
Regional Sports Council
RIBA
Messrs Riches
Shelagh Robinson (SJR)
FJ Rogers Ltd
Roundhay Churches
Royal Armouries Museum
Royal Mail
Rushbonds
Kenneth R Rutter
Salts Mill Estate
Salvation Army
Samaritans
Scattergood & Johnson
Diana Scott
Scurrah Wainwright Trust
Shadwell Horticultural Society
Mary Sheepshanks
Clare Short
Renee Silverman
Simpson Solk
Singer & Friedlander
Smith Devenish
Soroptomists International of Leeds
South Leeds Arts College
Gwen & Elizabeth Speak
St Annes Cathedral
St James University Hospital Trust
St Pauls, Ireland Wood
Stansfeld Steel
Stephen George and Partners
Sunstreet Printers
Sylvia Wright Trust
Cllr Neil Taggart (MICE)
Teesland Northern Developments Ltd
The Worshipful Company of Painters and Stainers
Theosophical Society

Thistle Hotels
Thoresby Society
Thorner & Roundhay Churches
Alan Titchmarsh
Touche Ross
Toulston Polo Club
Trinity and All Saints College
Trustees of Leeds General Infirmary
TSB
United Reformed Church
University of Leeds
University of Leeds Department of Textile Industries
University of Leeds Faculty of Medicine, Dentistry, Psychology and Health
Mrs Verity
Village Hotel & Leisure Club
Virgin Trains
Voluntary Action for Women
Voluntary Action Leeds
Bernadette Wade (OU)
Walker Morris
Wansbrough Willey Hargrave
Waterstones
Jean Watson
Weetwood Hall
West Yorkshire Federation of Women
Wheatfields Hospice
White Rose Guild of Lacemakers
Whitkirk Club
Wigton Moor Primary School
Claire Wildman
Willmott Dixon Construction Ltd
Women in Design & Contruction
Women in Management
Womens Institute
Wrens Association (WRVS)
Wrigleys Solicitors
WT Partnership
WYPTE
Yearly Accountancy
Yorkshire Arts
Yorkshire Bank plc
Yorkshire Chemicals plc
Yorkshire Cricket Club
Yorkshire Electricity
Yorkshire Enterprise
Yorkshire Environmental Consultants
Yorkshire Ladies Council of Education
Yorkshire Post Newspapers
Yorkshire Road Cycling Club
Yorkshire Television
Yorkshire Water
Arnold Ziff
Marjorie Ziff

Designed in collaboration with the Authors & Leeds Civic Trust by ehaw.
Printed by Hawthornes Printers.

Sponsors in Kind

A Childs Place
Addleshaw Booth & Co
Air UK
Armley Helping Hands
Armley Mills Industrial Museum
Lucy Aspinall
Bahai Faith Group
Gordon Bear
Bethel Day Centre
Bettys CafÈ
The Big Issue
Black Elders Association
Margaret Blakeborough
Bonds of Farsley
Christine Bowskill
Sheila Broun
CAFOD
Carey Jones
Casa Mia Restaurant, Chapel Allerton
CDW Ltd
Chapel Allerton Allotments Association
Chapel Allerton Festival
John Charles
Chinese Womens Group
Christian Aid

Chromagene
Clifford Brooke Centre
Brian Close
Andrew Cole
Peter Conolly
Angela Cooper
Eric Cowin
Crowne Plaza Hotel
Peter Crowther
Design Innovation Centre
DeVere Hotel
Drummonds
Mike Duffield
Ede & Ravenscroft
Fibre Optics FX
Jeanette Fleming
Shirley Gale
Gledhow Primary School
Valerie Gomersall
Greek Orthodox Church
Harehills Irish Music
Linda Harley
Harper Collins
Headingley Primary School
Jack Higgins
Hilton Hotel
Holy Trinity Cafe

Hotel Metropole
James Hare Silks
Jo Jevons
Joanna
Sue Kershaw
Kirkstall Valley Nature Reserve
Latch
Latin American Womens Support Group
Lou Lavender
Keely Laycock
Leeds Babies Welcome Association
Leeds Central Library
Leeds Chinese Community
Leeds City Council
Leeds Methodist Choir
Leeds Racial Equality Unit
Leeds Travellers Association
Lincoln Green Youth Base
Peter Lorimer
Madeira Threads
Paul Malkin
Marriott Hotel
Anita Mazzarella
Merrion Hotel
Miles Hill Primary School

Millrace Organic Restaurant
MKC Limited
Northern School of Contemporary Dance
Oxfam
Park Spring Primary School
Posthouse Hotel
Prudential Fund Managers
Queens Hotel
Louise Rabour
Maggie Rakusen
Rawdon Littlemoor School
Roscoe Luncheon Club
Samuel Taylor
Save The Children
Sir Jimmy Savile, OBE
Scott Hall & Sholebrooke Tenants Association
Serif Systems
Dianne Shillito
Skippko
Smallprint
South Parade Baptists
St Gemmas Hospice
St Marys High School
Jennifer Stead
Swarthmore Education Centre

Leeds Swordfish Appeal
Charlotte Taylor
Janet Taylor
The Grove Methodists
The Spice of Leeds
The Yarn Shop
Top Copy
Trade for Change
Traidcraft
Frankie Vaughan
Doran Waclawiak
Monica Walsh
Jean Watson
Wesley Road Chapel
West Yorkshire Playhouse
Westfield Junior School
William Witts Printers
John Williams
Simon Peter Wong
Woodhouse & Little London
Caring Together
Yorkshire Baptists
Yorkshire Dance
Yorkshire Television
Youth at Risk

Workshop Leaders

Diane Bates
Betty Bertrand
Ann Brown
Nicki Brown
Vivienne Brown
Clare Bryan
Freda Copley

Jane Dew
Caroline Dunn
Avtaar Flora
Maggie & Clive Grey
Sarah Hodgson
Sue Hodgson
Lizzie Ingle

Margaret Kenny
Paddy Killer
Joan Lister
Val Lloyd
Chris Richardson
Elaine Van Sante
Anna Sutcliffe

Denise Teed
Hilary Thurlow
Barbara Walker
Jamie Warren

Staff & Consultants

Staff

Sylvia Crowther - Fundraiser, Events Organiser and Minute Secretary

Consultants

Alan Carver
Andrew Cole
Paula Convy
Barbara Cresswell - Fundraiser 1995/96
Anne Croft
Gwen Howgate
Paddy Killer
Paul Malkin
Eric Marshall
Nicki Martineau - Fundraiser 1996/97

Rosie Kearton - Project Co-ordinator
Chris Ratcliffe
Brenda Rose
Kate Russell
Penny Stephenson
Liz Thorne
Jan Wells - Community Liason, Photographer
Jackie Wilkinson
Yearly Accountancy

Photographers

Martin Banks (Panels)
Kate Russell
Peter Wilson
Paul Wilkinson

Officers and Trustees

Trustees, Directors and Officers

NAME OF DIRECTOR OR MEMBER	DATE JOINED BOARD	DATE BECAME DIRECTOR	DATE RESIGNED FROM BOARD & AS DIRECTOR	NOTES
Betty Bertrand	17 Sep 1998	17 Sep 1998	-	Chair from Jan 2001
Eileen Cummings	13 May 2002	13 May 2002	-	Volunteer
Hilary Duncan	14 Jan 1997	-	13 Jul 1998	Not a Director
Glynis Evans	14 Jan 1997	-	13 Jul 1998	Not a Director
Gillian Holding	14 Jan 1997	-	-	Member from 14 Jan 1997
Jane Hustwit	14 Jan 1997	17 Sep 1998	20 Dec 2000	
James Johnson	14 Sep 2000	14 Sep 2000	8 Jul 2002	
Brenda Lancaster	22 Jan 2001	22 Jan 2001	-	
Cllr Graham Latty	20 Dec 2000	20 Dec 2000	13 Jun 2002	
Cllr Keith Loudon	14 Jan 1997	-	11 Sep 1998	Not a Director
Cllr Liz Minkin	14 Jan 1997	17 Sep 1998	20 Dec 2000	Chair to Dec 2000
Brian Peace	14 Jan 1997	14 Jan 1997	-	Company Secretary
Susan Pitter	22 Jan 2001	22 Jan 2001	-	
Kate Russell	14 Jan 1997	14 Jan 1997	-	Originator / Artistic Director
Bev Smalley OBE TD	3 Feb 1999	3 Feb 1999	10 Mar 2000	
Barbara Walker	15 Apr 2002	15 Apr 2002	-	Volunteer

OFFICERS	NAME	DATE APPOINTED	DATE RESIGNED
Honorary Secretary	**Brian Peace**	14 Jan 1997	-
Honorary Treasurer	Brian Peace	14 Jan 1997	11 May 1999
Honorary Treasurer	Fiona Meeson	11 May 1999	6 Jul 2000
Honorary Treasurer	**Esta Andrews**	11 Aug 2000	-
Minute Secretary	Sylvia Crowther	30 Mar 1998	30 Jun 2002

NOTES:

1. All acting Directors are Trustees of the Charity.
2. Current (October 2002) Trustees and Officers in **bold**.

The Process Continues

The authors and Trustees of the Tapestry wish to thank each and every person who has contributed to this project, whether or not they have a piece of embroidery on a panel or their name in the book. Many people called into a workshop and put a stitch in a panel but did not realise there was a register to sign. In some cases we have names of embroiderers and pieces but the two have become separated and cannot be matched.

It is the authors aim to identify every person who took part and record the information on an interactive web site which is currently being designed.

If you gave a donation of time or money or sponsored a section of embroidery and your name is not recorded in this book please contact Leeds Tapestry.

There is an enormous archive of research and design material together with letters and other documentation from the ten years of the project. This will be sitted through over the coming months and the useful information will be extracted for the web site. This archive will then be consigned to permanent storage.

There are over 1,200 names of individuals and organisations in the appendices at the end of this book. Many groups of individuals who were involved will be represented only by the name of the organisation. It would be great to have your names too!